THE NATIONAL HOME
INSPECTOR EXAMINATION

"HOW TO PASS ON YOUR FIRST TRY"!

By

Patrick J. Shepherd, P.E.

Thank you for purchasing The National Home Inspection Examination "How to Pass on Your First Try!" book. I know you could have picked any number of books for Exam prep, but you picked this one and for that I am extremely grateful.

The book was first published in 2016. I set out to write the book that I wish I had when I was preparing for this exam back in 2002- but never existed. Today, in 2023, we are still going strong. We work hard to keep the book updated and relevant to the constant changes to the exam format published by the national board.

I hope that this book adds value and quality to your exam preparation. If you enjoyed this book and found some benefits in using it to study for this exam, I'd like to hear from you and hope that you could take time to post a review on Amazon. Your feedback and support will help this author to greatly improve his writing craft for future projects and make this book even better.

Please leave an HONEST review.

Also, if you purchased the paperback on Amazon, please visit us on our Blog: https://howtopassthehomeinspectorexam.blogspot.com

Email us Here: EITFastTrack@gmail.com to receive a FREE Ebook version of this paperback!

We would love to hear from you!

Thank you.

TABLE OF CONTENTS:

Acres of Diamonds:

I heard an old tape recording of Earl Nightingale talking about this Acres of Diamonds story. It's awesome. It's a story of a farmer who heard tales about other farmers who had made millions by discovering diamond mines. He couldn't wait to sell his farm and go prospecting for diamonds himself. So, he sold his farm and spent the rest of his life looking for diamonds. However, he never did find them. Sadly, he died of old age and a broken heart.

Meanwhile, the person who bought his farm accidently discovered a small somewhat shiny object near the creek on his new property. He brought it to a jeweler who explained that it was a very small diamond. It just didn't look like a typical diamond because it wasn't polished yet. Well, he was so excited that he started mining his new land and discovered it contained millions of diamonds. It became the largest diamond mine in the world!

The moral of the story is that if the first farmer <u>had only taken the time to study and prepare himself</u> to learn what diamonds looked like in their rough state, and explore his property before looking elsewhere, he would have discovered the diamonds and riches he was searching for his entire life was in his own backyard.

We all have acres of diamonds already buried deep within ourselves, just waiting to be discovered. Before you run off exploring greener pastures, make sure that your own is not just as green or perhaps greener.

My Hope is that you take the time to study and prepare for this Exam. This is your first step to having a great career in Home Inspection. Don't just wing it. You probably already know most of the material, you just need to practice and follow some simple tips in order to bring out a passing score.

Welcome

Welcome Everyone!

Over the years, I developed a unique strategy to prepare for exams. As a student, I was always a great test taker. I developed a specific set of tips, strategies, and mindsets that help me perform well- not just on tests but also in life. I call this the Inner Game of Testing® and I would like to share it with you in this book.

Inner Game, in my opinion, is the most important thing you need. The Inner Game takes place within your mind and starts long before you even show up to take the test. It is played against such obstacles as fear, self-doubt, uncertainty, and limiting beliefs. The Inner Game is being played in your head before you ever go out into the world and take action.

Inner Game of Testing:

In my experience, the concept of Inner Game was never taught in school. If it were, I missed it. I believe it allows you to use your thoughts and beliefs to assist you on obtaining your goals. There are two major games that we must play in life. The first one is called the "outer game" and the second one is called the "inner game". The inner game is where it all begins.

Rarely does your best performance come out when we need it

That's why sports teams play the game. If there were no chance of the weaker team winning, why even play? Doesn't the better team always win? No!

Look at the following equation:

Performance = Potential – Interference

I want to show you how to minimize the "Interference" variable in the equation above. By doing so, it tips the odds in your favor so you can anchor yourself into a peak state of certainty, clarity, confidence, and courage during the test. It allows your best-self and performance to come through because you don't have to deal with all the bullsh$t (I mean interference). If you don't minimize the interference, it will affect your performance.

In life, interference can be things like hanging out with the wrong crowd, smoking, doing drugs, unhealthy eating habits, not setting goals, low level of standards, etc. Anything that prevents you from being your best-self and accomplishing your goals.

But with taking the Home Inspector Exam, <u>Interference</u> can be:

- Not arriving 30 minutes early to the test center and all the parking spots are already filled up. You get frustrated and lose your focus.

- Not knowing that you need to pay for parking, and you don't have cash. You get really frustrated.

- Having study habits that suck. You don't realize that this is all about developing problem recognition skills. You just need to put in the work upfront to be able to identify them. All you need to do is study a collection of solved problems in each category. That is what this book is about.

- Listening to a bunch of Debby Downers® right before the exam which affects your mood. Ignore the naysayers. No one has ever erected a statue for a critic.

- Not having any systems in place to help keep you on an effective study track. You just aimlessly work a problem or two a few times per week. You have no schedule set up, no dedicated study space and you leave it all up to chance. Let's see how that works out for you. How you do anything is how you do everything. You need to take this exam seriously and don't be lazy.

- Spending too much time on the harder problems and thinking that you must go in sequential order. You waste all your time. You don't realize there is low hanging fruit in the back of the exam, and you run out of time before you get to them.

- Not realizing that you can make up in numbers what you lack in skill. You don't have to be the smartest Home Inspector; you just need to work more practice problems. Success is always at the margins! The little extra things you do to prepare makes all the difference.

- Not trusting that the Law of Averages will work out in your favor. You allow small setbacks to rob you of opportunities because you quit when times get rough.

- Not disciplining your disappointments. You allow yourself to become frustrated during the exam because you feel like you're getting a lot wrong. You only need to get about 65% correct in order to pass. Progress > Perfection.

- You don't practice the Second Effort. You don't give 100% on every problem because you don't realize that it only comes down to a few questions that, if answered correctly, will make you pass. This separates the winners from the losers.

- Not being comfortable with getting 4 out of 10 questions wrong. You will still pass with just over 60% correct.

- Not preparing the recommended 8 weeks before the exam.

- Not playing the percentages nor choosing a good pitch to swing at.

- You wasted too much time trying to figure outed hard questions during the exam. This is a big one.

- Not using the process of elimination. Just by eliminating 1 or 2 possible choices greatly improves your odds at guessing the correct one.

- Letting the test takers inside your head. Don't let the bastards get you down!

- Flipping through the questions in this book for the first time and becoming discouraged. It doesn't represent everything that you need to know, but only what could possibly show up on the exam. Just means that everything in it is Fair Game – just know where to find it. Don't have to be an expert at it.

- Posting your goals on social media -only for the validation. But you never had any real intentions on following through with it. Don't do it. Post after you pass. Under promise, over deliver.

- Not relaxing the day before the test. Don't get drunk either. Drink after you pass.

- Not having a Razor's Edge working for you. The line between winning and losing, passing or failing, is extremely thin. **Success is always at the margins.** My Razor's Edge when I took this exam was that I worked more practice problems than anyone else. Morning, noon, and night. Find your Razor's Edge.

- Not setting yourself up for success. Your personal philosophy and set of the sail sucks. Not having any goals you are working towards that pull you into the future. You're in the 97% group that aren't even trying. Join the 3%.

- Not realizing that opportunities are often disguised as work.

- Not eating healthy and regularly exercising.

- Not understanding that you must get in the proper "learning" mindset and realize that this test is an opportunity to develop new skills. No matter how hard it is at first, you'll be able to improve over time through hard work and practice.

- Not realizing your score will reflect the amount of work you put in - not just your raw intelligence.

- Not realizing that you must build speed, since you're battling the clock more than the complexity of the exam.

- Not understanding that you can create your own luck. When you take care of the little things, most things just tend to go your way. It's just the way it is. Cause and Effect. Luck is when opportunity meets with preparation.

- Not hanging up a blank certificate frame. Don't do it, I don't care. But it absolutely works and will motivate you.

- Not knowing that you can mold your Self Image into anything you want. Great test taker, public speaker, etc.! It's time to upgrade your software by increasing the set point in your own mind.

- Not realizing that you already have Acres of Diamonds buried within yourself just waiting to be discovered and polished. It's not "out there", it's within you.

- Not setting up a finite schedule for studying. Something will take as much time as you allow for it. Set a very specific time and ending for study. If it's an open block of time, you will fill it up with procrastination until that time is up.

- Skipping batting practice. You need to practice at solving these problems. Why do you think the best baseball hitters of all time still had to take batting practice before every game? They're already good, why the need for practice? Because they need to warm up, there's a certain way to hit a fastball, curve ball, or a changeup. Batters are trained to look at the spin of the ball as it leaves the pitcher's hand, they are getting focused, working on their swing, working on their inner game, etc. Just like you should work all these different types of problems, be on the lookout for patterns, knowing how to answer these questions. You need to take batting practice before the big game.

- Feeling frustrated during the exam from the feeling that there just wasn't enough time to finish the test. It is supposed to be that way. It's completely normal. This Exam is designed to be hard and not being able to finish. Care less. Get 4 out of 10 questions wrong and you will still pass. They purposely make some really hard questions to see if you're smart enough to skip them. You don't get any extra points for solving them. They are testing to see if you are smart enough to skip them.

- Not studying the format of the exam and knowing what to expect.

- Not studying the main topic areas on your exam and what types of question to expect. The greatest chess players of all-time study their opponent's opening repertoire, tendencies, habits, strengths and weaknesses, etc. They don't just show up and play chess. Same with pro sports.

- Not knowing ahead of time how many minutes per problem you have on average. That's sad. You need to have an internal gauge in your mind constantly monitoring it. Spending too much time? Skip.

- Not checking to see if your felt marker works when you sit at the testing table. Trust me on this one.

- Not realizing that your criteria for success should be if you are taking action each day. Not solving all the practice problems correctly.

There. I just summed up the entire book for you. If you can eliminate all the bullsh$t interreference ahead of time, it will allow you to be in a flow state. None of these things take any skill to do- they're very easy to do.

Hang up a Blank Certificate Frame:

(The Vacuum Law of Prosperity)

I learned this from Bob Proctor. This might sound really silly, but the first thing you need to do is to go buy a blank certificate frame and hang it up on the wall where you can see it every day.

Imagine that you already passed this exam and are now looking at the passing certificate in its frame. How does it feel? What does passing mean to you? Perhaps it means ultimate success for all your hard work. A real sense of encompassment. Feel how proud you are and what it took to achieve this goal. Look at it and visualize it every day. I used this technique many times in my life and it works. It sounds crazy but it's effective and motivating. Ask any Olympic athlete if they use visualization. They do.

The Vacuum Law of Prosperity says that the fastest way to manifest something in your life is to create a vacuum. By creating a vacuum and creating space, you allow your vision or goal to show up. But you must first create that space for it to manifest into reality. Visualization plays an important role. I use this all the time. If you can see it, it can happen -because your inner world creates your outer world. Your physical world is just a printout of your inner world. Everything comes from thoughts. Once you decide to create space, nature has no choice but to adhere a vacuum. Like pulling a plunger out, it creates negative pressure - a vacuum. As the volume increases, air rushes in to fill the void.

Do you want to create a successful business? The first step is to get a manilla folder and label it "New Business". There you go- it's a start. Want to pass a test? Hang up a blank certificate frame. Want a new wardrobe? Clean out the old clothes first. Want to write a book? Create a new document and name it "New Book". Want fresh and exciting new ideas? Let go of your old ones. That's the first step. Nature has no choice but to fill the empty space. Of course, you must follow it up with action.

How This Book Works

The problem with most home inspection exam study materials is that they do not teach you how to pass the exam. They contain many different types of questions -ranging from too general to very unrealistic problems- which only waste your time. They tend to deal with too much theory and outdated codes, and the study material ultimately ends up being a book of random practice problems. Our book covers virtually all the home inspection-related topics on the exam as well as non-inspection related test topics.

We believe that the best way to prepare for this exam is to develop a specific strategy to pass it. Our curriculum follows the identical content outline of the National Home Inspector Examination which is published by the national board of home inspectors. In order to pass the home inspector exam, it is not necessary to study everything, but only a fraction of each subject. The book will show you how to maximize your score.

Our book is designed *specially* to teach you how to pass the exam. This book contains over 400 practice problems compiled into (6) Exams. The questions are very similar to those on the National Home Inspector Examination and a significant percentage of the questions were from previous exams. The NHIE exam is very difficult and has a high failure rate. This book does not waste time on theory or outdated problems- which will only confuse you more, but instead, only contains practical questions and ones that are _most likely_ to appear on the actual exam based on the percentages which are published by the Examination Board of Professional Home Inspectors.

Our research team consists of licensed home inspectors, professional engineers, and expert contractors and tradesmen. Our question developers and researchers, collectively, have hundreds of years of experience and success in the home inspection profession. The problems were developed using the examination board's percentage breakdowns on each topic area and are presented in a logical order which will allows you to master the relevant information. This book will serve as your game plan for exam day. Never again will you have to use multiple resources when studying for this examination.

By utilizing the percentages from Examination Board of Professional Home Inspectors, the book maximizes your exposure to all problem types in shortest amount of time. And by eliminating obscure and outdated problem types, this book contains only realistic problems and provides excellent practice to prepare you for the actual exam. We believe that nothing prepares you better than working through actual exam questions. Most home inspection training schools provide you with multiple reference textbooks and information. After the classroom requirement is over, they leave it all up to you to study for the national exam. Our book is the only resource that you will need to pass the exam.

Many experienced and knowledgeable contractors, who are eager to branch into the home inspection business, consistently make the common mistake of underestimating the Home Inspector Examination. While they may be very knowledgeable in different trades, they fail to realize that the exam is based on very specific standards and industry codes. In addition, practicing home inspectors wishing to become licensed can also have a hard time passing the exam- even though they have been in the profession for a long period of time- because they don't properly prepare for the exam. Engineers who want to become home inspectors without any formal training also have a high failure rate.

A qualified home inspector must master a number of subjects and have a keen eye and acquire specialized knowledge. Successful examiners must have a working knowledge of the various codes, inspection methods, building systems, exterior systems, structural systems, roofing systems, electrical systems, heating and cooling systems, insulating and ventilating systems, plumbing systems, interior systems, and fireplace and chimney systems, and professional practice. This book serves as the transition from other professional (building trades, engineering) over to home inspections. Everything home inspectors do is based on the building codes. For this reason, the home inspector must know building codes in addition to looking for defects in a home and also identify the building materials present by their defining characteristics. This book will prepare you in all the relevant knowledge areas are covered in the exam.

This book contains over 400 practice problems compiled in (6) exams. The questions will guide you through each section of the exam content so you can learn how every chapter is organized. The exams are organized in random topic order, simulating the actual exam, allowing you to hone your skills in solving many types of problems thrown at you from all directions. However, since every question in the book is categorized by topic in the table provided on page 21, you have to option of working on any specific topic if you choose. For example, if you know that your weak area is "Electrical", use the specification chart to find out which question numbers are electrical type problems. Flip straight to them and start working.

This book systematically forces you to work through each of the topic areas and only focus on topics with the highest percentage of showing up on the actual exam. The method used in this book allows you to study at your own pace, when and where it's convenient for you. You will learn all of the major systems and components found in residential construction. Don't waste your time any longer! You need to start working problems.

The 2022 Exam Format

The National Home Inspector Examination contains 200 multiple-choice questions. You are given four hours to complete the exam. The exam is administered nationwide by a testing company at 250 proctored test center locations throughout the United States. Please check your state rules to learn how to register. The exam is available at any time of the year when the testing center you select is open for business and has seats available. Advance registration is required.

The National Home Inspector Examination fee is $225 per test. You will receive one copy of your official passing score sheet before you leave the testing center. The passing score sheet will show your score on a scale of 200-800, with 500 as the pass point. The failing score sheet will show a graph of your performance in each content area of the examination. You will receive your official score sheet with unique identification number and digital photo at the end of the examination. It's your responsibility to follow through with the appropriate authority in your state.

What to bring?

- Your confirmation number

- Two forms of signature identification, one of which must be photo-bearing, preferably a driver's license

- Your failing score report, if you are retaking the examination

Please note, if you do not present all of the above items on examination day or if you are late, you may be denied admission to the test and considered absent. You will owe the full examination fee.

Don't be late!

Computer Based Testing Strategy

1) It is highly recommended that you do the short tutorial at the beginning of the exam on your computer prior to beginning the exam. It will teach you how to navigate through the questions, and more importantly, how to mark/flag a question in order to come back to it later. If you have basic computer skills, you will be tempted to skip over the tutorial because it will seem self-explanatory, however, it will be time well spent. Part of your overall exam strategy, which is covered in the next section, will be to mark/flag the harder questions for a later time when you make your second pass. It also shows you how to activate the clock/timer which tracks how much time is remaining on your exam. If you skip the tutorial, you are risking not knowing how to navigate the software. Take this time to relax and go through the short tutorial at the beginning of the exam.

2) Paper and pencils will not be allowed in the testing centers and which also includes scratch sheets to work out problems. All examinees will be provided with dry-erase booklets for problem solving. Expect the booklet to be a spiral bound (at the top) laminated notebook with dimensions slightly larger than a sheet of loose-leaf paper. It will be made up of about ten laminated sheets.

3) You will be provided with a fine-tipped marker which will be about the size and weight of a standard ink pen. As soon as you receive it at your work center, remember to **test it** on the laminated notebook in order to verify that it works! You will be surprised that a majority of the dry erase markers will be low on ink, and you do not want to begin your exam only to realize that your pen doesn't work when you reached the first problem where you have to calculate something! The test centers see hundreds of examiners per day (not just home inspection examiners) and it really just comes down to one person overseeing the test center. The last thing on their mind is to change out pens, especially while they are responsible for monitoring the entire center. Test your markers; you will be happy that you did.

4) When you are faced with a harder type question which you do not recognize the solution to be immediately solvable, we recommend flagging (skipping) the question in order to go to the next question. You learn how to do this from the tutorial at the beginning. But since this is a computer based test, you cannot write notes in the exam booklet. However, you can write notes in small print at top or back of any page

in the laminated notebook. Let's say that you can't remember the code for a stair landing in order to solve a particular question, you should write the question # and page # (and any notes to yourself) on the back of the last page of the laminate notebook so you can save time when you come back to it at later.

6) We highly recommend that you double check that the clock/timer is activated in the lower right side of the screen before you begin the exam. The timer tells you how much time is remaining on your test. You learn this in the tutorial at the beginning of the exam. It will appear at the bottom right side of your computer screen. However, sometimes you must manually activate it before you begin. Be sure to monitor it as you are answering questions to gage how fast or how slow you are going. Remember, since this is a computer-based exam, there will be no proctor telling you how much time you have remaining on your exam, it is entirely up to you to regularly monitor your time throughout the exam.

8) We strongly suggest wearing the earmuffs (sound proofing) which will be provided for you at your computer terminal. Please realize that not all examiners in the test center are taking the same exam as you. Some examiners are there for different reasons; such as, continuing education courses, company screening testing, driver's education, etc. Therefore, not examiners take their exams seriously and may tend make a lot of noise (by eating snacks, listening to music, etc.) at their computer terminal. But this is not you! The home inspector examination is the first step for you to beginning your career. You are taking this test seriously. In order to drown out background noise and distractions, as soon as you begin the tutorial, you should put on the earmuffs. Once the test begins, you will not even realize that you have them on.

9) The testing center will be very strict about not bringing any cell phones, personal items, etc. into the testing center. If you do bring personal items in, they will have a locker for you to lock them up in before you will be allowed to enter the area where the computer terminals are located. You will need to lock up your keys, wallet, etc. in the locker. We suggest leaving all other items, including cell phones, in your car. Do not bring anything with you into the test center other than your license and test center confirmation code/paperwork (which you print out after you register with the test center). You worked too hard to get to this point to risk getting caught with your cell phone in your pocket and having your exam disqualified on the spot. Just leave it in

your car. You have the rest of your life to look at your cell phone. Don't bring it with you.

10) You will not be allowed to study in the testing center while waiting for your test to begin. They will make you leave the waiting area if they see you studying. Therefore, it is best to sit in your car upon arriving at the test center until about 30 minutes prior to test time. Spend this time flipping through this book one last time, reviewing questions, and focusing on your game plan. Be sure to read your confirmation page that you printed out from the testing center, it may require you to check in at least 20 minutes prior to your scheduled test time. **Don't be late!**

11) Visit the testing center's website to learn more about their requirements. Learn the directions to the test center, parking arrangements (do you need money to park?) which floor is the center located on? You want to eliminate all possible distractions on exam day so you can focus on what you have to do.

Overall Testing Strategy

The national average for the pass rate of this exam is in the mid 60% range. You should not underestimate this exam. If you study the problems in this book and have an open mind to learn then you can pass. The test will not be **difficult** if you know the material. Take time and effort to prepare correctly. Take a copy of book with you and read problems throughout the day. Develop of habit of reading a few questions in the morning, lunchtime, and in the evenings. Studying in small increments throughout the day will add up overtime.

The exam tests basic common knowledge that any home inspector should know. Most of us do not give ourselves enough credit for knowing a lot of stuff. You would be surprised just how much you know and on the other hand how much you don't know. But you have to study for this exam – you cannot just wing it.

You will find that most of the questions in this book are relatively easy to solve. This is on **purpose**! Most of the problems on the actual home inspector exam will be easy to solve. There will be some hard questions, but you do not get any extra points for solving the harder problems. Remember, your goal to pass the exam, you do not need to score a 100%. In reality, you only need around 65% in order to pass. Since the board determines the cut score for each exam, no one knows exactly what the score is since it is determined specifically for each session. Some questions get thrown out if a lot of people miss them. Therefore, you are not only completing against yourself but against other test takers. You should only focus on maximizing your points. You accomplish this by **not wasting precious time trying to solve harder problems.** There will be a lot of easy questions on the test, but if you waste time solving the challenging ones, you will run out of time to solve the easy ones which could be at the end of the test.

As major league baseball fans, we tend to quote Ted Williams to take takers in our prep classes in order to make the comparison to the perfect test taker. Ted was arguably the greatest pure hitter who ever lived and he was the first to bring math and statistics into the game of baseball. In his book, The Science of Hitting, Ted explains how to play percentages. He knew the strike zone and disciplined himself not to swing at balls outside it. "Get a good pitch to hit" was the mantra taught to him by Rogers Hornsby, the batting instructor for Minneapolis. By being selective and by learning how to only swing at high percentage pitches, he has one of the highest batting averages ever in the history of baseball. Ted became legendary for his patience at the plate.

It is our desire in writing this book to teach take takers the art of playing the percentages in order to maximize their score when taking this exam. We show you why you should be patient while taking the test and how to search out and find those high percentage questions to answer. Just as Ted Williams only swung at the high percentage pitches, we show you how to identify high percentage pitches (easy and medium questions) on the test and not waste time on outside pitches (hard questions). **You will learn that only spending time on the questions that matter is the key to scoring high**. Take takers will learn that perfect practice is the key.

We hope that you practice the example problems in this book- they continue to appear time and time again on the actual exam. Follow the tips and advice in this book and you will pass on your first try.

The overall strategy that we recommend is based on the 80/20 principle. The 80/20 principle is named after the Italian economist Vilfredo Pareto, who observed that 80% of income in Italy was received by 20% of the Italian population. The assumption is that most of the results in any situation are determined by a small number of causes and that 80 percent of your outcomes come from 20 percent of your inputs. There are business examples such as 20 percent of employees are responsible for 80 percent of a company's output or 20 percent of customers are responsible for 80 percent of the revenues. You may also notice how you may only wear 20% of the clothes in your closet 80% of the time!

The important thing to understand is that in your life there are certain activities you do (your 20 percent) that account for the majority (your 80 percent) of your happiness and outputs. When you start to analyze and breakdown your life into elements it's very easy to see 80/20 ratios all over the place. The trick, once your key happiness determinants have been identified, is to make everything work in harmony and avoid wasting time on those 80 percent activities that produce little satisfaction for you.

The message is simple enough – **focus on activities that produce the best outcomes for you.**

Many take takers do not get their best possible score because they waste precious time on hard questions. They simply just run out of time and do not get a chance to answer the easy and medium questions that remained. Time management plays an important factor during the test. You don't need to answer all of the questions right to do well. You only need to answer about 65% of the questions right in order to pass! So if you know you aren't going to be able to finish the exam, you can actually focus on just about 65 percent of the questions, and if you get a good amount of them right (and make sure you still use the last few minutes to guess on the rest) you will pass.

Take takers often tell us that there just wasn't enough time to finish the test, and we always tell them, **"It is supposed to be that way!"** It's completely normal. The exam is designed to be hard and not being able to finish. Do not panic. Go in with the number of questions you need to answer to achieve your goal score then in the last minute or two, guess on the rest, and you will likely get some of those right, which will only raise your score. If there is a question you don't know the answer to, or you know will take a long time to answer correctly, simply just skip it.

The test intentionally contains questions that the test developers know will take a lot of time to answer. Don't fall into their traps. Skip the really tough ones, and if you have time, come back to them, or just guess when you are using your last minute or two to fill in all of the questions. The exam has questions that are not only difficult, but also take a lot of time to answer. **They are testing whether you are smart enough to skip these questions.** Many take takers do not skip hard questions, but instead, waste quality time and still end up getting it wrong.

Using the 80/20 principle as a tool allows you to spend the most amount of time on the problems that matter - **the easy and medium questions.** We handpicked all of the example problems in this book based on the 80/20 rule – all of which have a high percentage chance of showing up on the exam. In order to maximize your score, you have to search out and find the easy and medium questions and answer those first. Find the "low hanging fruit" type questions first. This strategy allows you to now have 1.8 minutes per question to answer questions as opposed to 1 minute per question. In the last 2 minutes remaining in each section, you can make an educated guess on all the harder type questions. Using this method, you give yourself an extra 39 seconds to focus on each question. Even with a few careless errors— don't set yourself up for perfection—you'll be far more accurate than trying to answer every single question perfectly.

For some reason, the idea that you have to work every single problem correctly gets passed on from generation to generation. It's a vicious cycle. No one is perfect. Hall of Famers, the best baseball hitters of all time, only hit the ball 30% of the time (3 out of 10 times at bat). Conversely, this means they failed 70% of the time. Think about it. The best hitters in history never hit the ball in 7 out of 10 at bats. Don't pressure yourself for perfection, keep it all in perspective.

Remember, we are trying to play percentages here. You are not only competing against yourself; you are also competing against all the other test takers on test day. **On test day, let all the other test takers waste time trying to solve all the hard problems in sequential order** while you stick to your strategy. There are only 2 things that you have control over on this test: 1) How much time you allot to each question, and 2) How you prepare and practice ahead of time. You must manage your time effectively by following the strategies in this book. You will maximize your score by focusing on about 65% of the test questions and answering correctly than attempting to solve every question in the section perfectly.

You should only focus on maximizing your points. You accomplish this by **not wasting precious time trying to solve harder problems.** There will be a lot of easy questions on the exam, but if you waste time solving the challenging ones, you will run out of time to solve the easy ones which will be at the end of the test. You need to maximize your time.

Here's how you do it: It is broken down into 3 steps (passes)

On your FIRST PASS, only solve the easier problems first. If you read a question and immediately know the answer then go ahead and solve it. However, if at first when you read the question and you don't IMMEDIATELY know how to solve it, then mark/flag it and skip to the next question. You learn how to flag a question in the short tutorial at the beginning of the test. Most of your FIRST PASS strategy should be able to find questions that are basic and easy to solve. It will be perfectly normal to skip the first 10-20 questions using this strategy, but remember, you are trying to maximize your points. You don't need to solve all of the questions in exact order in exact order. Don't worry about how many questions that you are skipping. Less experience test takers will be struggling and wasting their time on these harder questions in the beginning while you are answering all the easy questions. Your FIRST PASS is all about answering the "low hanging fruit" types of questions. There will be a lot of them scattered through the exam, the trick is having the patience to skip through the test in order to find them. Go find them and rack up easy points.

On your SECOND PASS, quickly review any notes that you made to yourself in the laminated booklet to see if you can now answer any questions that you first skipped. Don't waste a lot of time on problems that you still have no idea how to solve. Remember, a lot of the questions will only require a few short steps to solve, so if the problem appears to be very complex, there is a good chance that there could be extra information in the problem that you do not need in order to solve. Try reading it over and over to try to narrow it down to specifically what they are asking. If you are spending too much time on a particular question, just skip it and go on to the next question. The SECOND PASS is really an iterative approach where you are looking into the problems a little deeper trying to find the correct answer. Do not randomly guess at this point unless you are confident the answer is correct. If there is any time left at the end of the test then the difficult problems can be addressed.

The THIRD PASS begins about 5 minutes prior to the end of the test. Keep an eye on the little timer/clock in the bottom right hand corner of the screen; be sure it is turned on! Try to determine if you can eliminate one possible answer choice based on professional judgment. If you just totally guess outright, you have a 25% chance of guessing correctly. But if you can eliminate just one answer choice, you then just increased your odds at guessing correctly by 8%! Eliminate 2 answer choices; you now have a 50% chance of guessing correctly. Using this strategy, if you have 15 questions remaining when time is running out, you should at least, based on the odds, guess 3 or 4 correctly. If you can eliminate a few choices, you may be able to guess 7 or 8 correctly - which may be enough to pass the cut score. **Do not leave any question blank!** There is no penalty for guessing. Don't just guess, make an educated guess and use good judgment. You can get a lot of questions down to 2 or 3 answers choices by inspection.

Unofficially, you only need about 65% to pass this exam. Concentrate on the problems you know something about. Guess quickly on the rest.

Train for a good 6 weeks, getting comfortable reading the problems and understanding the solutions.

You must build speed, since you're battling the clock more than the complexity of the exam.

Most of the problems on the exam do not require a lot of work. The exam is testing your knowledge of basic topics. If a problem seems really difficult, look for a simple and easy way to solve.

Be sure to read the questions slowly and pay attention to if it says all of the following are types of heat pumps, except. Be sure to choose the one that isn't a heat pump. The problem could ask you to choose one of the following that is a type of footing. In this case, only one answer will be a type of footing.

Exam Content Outline

What' is covered in the National Home Inspector Examination?

The exam breakdown is split into 3 performance domains with specific tasks associated with each domain.

The Content Outline includes:

(Note: The percentage of questions from each Performance Domain is included)

I) PERFORMANCE DOMAIN I: BUILDING SCIENCE (37%)

Task 1: Identify and inspect site conditions using applicable standards for material selection and installation procedures to assess immediate and long-term safety and maintenance issues that can affect the building or people.

a. Vegetation, Grading, Drainage, and Retaining Walls

b. Driveways, Patios, and Walkways

c. Decks, Balconies, Stoops, Stairs, Steps, Porches, and Applicable Railings

Task 2: Identify and inspect building exterior components using applicable standards for material selection and installation procedures to assess immediate and long-term safety and maintenance issues that can affect the performance of the building.

a. Wall Cladding, Flashing, Trim, Eaves, Soffits, and Fascia

b. Exterior Doors and Windows

c. Roof Coverings

d. Roof Drainage Systems

---

e. Flashings

f. Skylights and Other Roof Penetrations

Task 3: Identify and inspect **structural system** elements using applicable standards for material selection and installation procedures to assess immediate and long-term safety and maintenance issues that may affect the structural stability of the building.

a. Foundation

b. Floor Structure

c. Walls and Vertical Support Structures

d. Roof and Ceiling Structures

Task 4: Identify and inspect electrical system elements using applicable standards for material selection and installation procedures to assess immediate and long-term safety and maintenance issues.

a. Service Drop of Service Lateral, Service Equipment, and Service Grounding

b. Interior Components of Service Panels and Subpanels

c. Wiring Systems

d. Devices, Equipment, and Fixtures (e.g., switches, receptacles, lights)

Task 5: Identify and inspect cooling systems using applicable standards for material selection and installation procedures to assess immediate and long-term safety and maintenance issues that may affect the performance of the building.

a. Cooling

b. Distribution Systems

c. Venting Systems

Task 6: Identify and inspect heating systems using applicable standards for material selection and installation procedures to assess immediate and long-term safety and maintenance issues that may affect the performance of the building.

a. Heating

b. Distribution Systems

c. Combustion Venting Systems

Task 7: Identify and inspect insulation and attic/crawl space ventilation systems using applicable standards for material selection and installation procedures to assess immediate condition and long-term safety and maintenance issues that may affect the performance of the building.

a. Thermal Insulation

b. Moisture Management

c. Ventilation Systems of Attics, Crawl Spaces, Roof Assemblies, and Interior Spaces

Task 8: Identify and inspect plumbing systems using applicable standards for material selection and installation procedures to assess immediate and long-term safety and maintenance issues that may affect the performance of the building.

a. Water Supply Distribution System

b. Fixtures and Faucets

c. Drain, Waste, and Vent Systems

d. Water Heating Systems

e. Fuel Storage and Fuel Distribution Systems

f. Safety issues, applicable standards, and appropriate terminology

Task 9: Identify and inspect interior components using applicable standards for material selection and installation procedures to assess immediate and long-term safety and maintenance issues that may affect the performance of the building.

a. Walls, Ceiling, Floors, Doors, and Windows

b. Walls, Ceiling, Floors, Doors, Windows, and Related

c. Steps, Stairways, Landings, and Railings

d. Installed Countertops and Cabinets

e. Garage Doors and Operators

Task 10: Identify and inspect fireplace and chimney systems using applicable standards for material selection and installation procedures to assess immediate and long-term safety and maintenance issues that may affect performance of the building.

a. Fireplaces, Solid-Fuel Burning Appliances, Chimneys, and Vents

Task 11: Identify and inspect common permanently installed kitchen appliances to determine if the on-off controls operate.

a. Installation methods

b. Operating using normal controls

c. Typical defects

d. Maintenance concerns and procedures

e. Safety issues, applicable standards, and appropriate terminology

Task 12: Identify and inspect pool and spa systems using applicable standards for material selection and installation procedures to assess immediate and long-term safety and maintenance issues.

a. Identify type of construction

b. Mechanical systems
c. Electrical systems

d. Typical defects

e. Maintenance concerns and procedures

f. Safety issues, applicable standards, and appropriate terminology

Task 13: Identify and inspect lawn irrigation systems using applicable standards for material selection and installation procedures to assess immediate and long-term safety and maintenance issues that may affect the performance of the system and building.

a. Common water distribution types, materials, applications, installation methods, and construction techniques

b. Typical modifications, repairs, upgrades, and retrofits methods and materials

c. Typical defects (e.g., cross-connection, back flow)

d. Common water pressure/flow problems and how they affect the water distribution system

e. Pipe deterioration issues (e.g., PVC, galvanized, brass)

f. Maintenance concerns and procedures

g. Safety issues, applicable standards, and appropriate terminology

II) PERFORMANCE DOMAIN II: ANALYSIS AND REPORTING (41%)

Task 1: In the inspection report, identify building systems and components by their distinguishing characteristics (e.g., type, size, location) to inform the client what was inspected.

a. Minimum information required in an inspection report (e.g., property data, construction materials, installation techniques, locations of main system shut-offs)

b. Describing the type of systems and the location of system components

c. Correct technical terms to describe systems and components of the building

Task 2: Describe inspection methods and limitations in the inspection report to inform the client what was not inspected.

a. Minimum and critical information required in an inspection report (e.g., weather conditions, inspection safety limitations, components not accessible)

b. Common methods used to inspect particular components (e.g., roofs, attics, sub-floor crawl spaces, mechanical components)

Task 3: Describe systems and components inspected that are not functioning properly or
are otherwise defective in comparison to the accepted norm.

a. Common expected service life of building and mechanical components

b. Common safety hazards

c. Common test instruments and their proper use for qualitative analysis (e.g., moisture meters, CO meters, probes)

Task 4: List recommendations to correct deficiencies or items needing further evaluation.

a. Correct professional or tradesperson required to effect repairs or perform further evaluations

b. Common remedies for correction

c. Relationships between components in the building

d. When to immediately inform building occupants of a life threatening safety hazard (e.g., gas leak, carbon monoxide accumulation)

III) PERFORMANCE DOMAIN III: BUSINESS OPERATIONS (21%)

Task 1: Identify the elements of the written inspection contract (e.g., scope, limitations, terms of services) to establish the rights and responsibilities of the inspector and client.

a. Purpose of a contract

b. Elements of a contract

c. Timing

d. Accepted standards of practice

e. Dispute resolution options

Task 2: Identify conflicts of interest to the client (e.g., inspector interest in the property, third-party stakeholders with financial interest in the outcome of the inspection).

a. Potential conflicts of interest involving parties other than the client

b. Potential conflicts between client and inspector

c. Relationships with other business professionals (e.g., engineers, contractors, building officials, realty agents, appraisers, lenders)

Task 3: Identify responsibilities to the client in order to maintain the quality, integrity, reputation, and objectivity of the inspection process while protecting the client's interests.

The chart on the following page categorizes each question into topic area:

10 Topic Areas:	Question # in this Book:
1) Communication and Professional Practice	1, 2, 12, 18, 19, 20, 23, 25, 29, 44, 51, 60, 63, 80, 82, 83, 84, 85, 86, 87, 88, 89, 90, 91, 118, 132, 136, 144,
2) Exteriors	3, 6, 10, 16, 31, 40, 43, 46, 52, 62, 64, 70, 71, 92, 94, 97, 99, 114, 138, 147, 196, 197, 200, 201, 202, 255, 256, 257, 258, 259, 260, 261, 262, 263, 264, 265, 266, 267, 268, 269, 270, 271, 272, 273, 274, 275, 276, 277, 278, 282, 283, 284, 285, 286,
3) Roofing	22, 42, 57, 95, 98, 102, 104, 105, 106, 107, 108, 109, 110, 112, 113, 146, 225, 226, 227, 228, 229, 230, 231, 232, 233, 234, 235, 236, 237, 238, 239, 240, 241, 242, 243, 244, 245, 246, 247, 248, 249, 250, 394, 395,
4) Structure	9, 13, 14, 24, 30, 36, 45, 48, 58, 59, 68, 69, 100, 101, 103, 115, 116, 117, 120, 121, 122, 123, 124, 125, 126, 139, 140, 141, 145, 253, 254, 279, 280, 281, 287, 288, 289, 290, 291, 292, 293, 294, 295, 296, 396, 397, 398, 399,
5) Insulation	8, 34, 54, 93, 96, 127, 129, 133, 299, 349, 350, 351, 352, 353, 354, 355, 356, 357, 358, 374, 375, 376, 377, 378, 379, 380, 381, 382, 383, 384, 385, 386, 387, 388, 389, 390, 391, 392, 393
6) Interiors	4, 15, 17, 26, 28, 38, 111, 148, 251, 252, 315, 316, 317, 318, 319, 320, 321, 346, 347, 348, ,
7) Electrical Systems	5, 27, 33, 35, 47, 49, 50, 53, 76, 149, 150, 151, 152, 153, 154, 155, 156, 157, 158, 159, 160, 297, 298, 300, 301, 302, 303, 304, 305, 306, 307, 308, 309, 310, 311, 312, 313, 314,400
8) Heating	21, 55, 72, 73, 77, 128, 131, 137, 161, 162, 163, 164, 165, 166, 167, 168, 169, 170, 171, 172, 175, 176, 177, 178, 179, 180, 181, 182, 183, 184, 186, 187, 188, 189, 190, 191, 193, 194, 195, 199, 322, 323,324, 325, 326,
9) Cooling	7, 11, 61, 78, 130, 134, 135, 203, 204, 205, 206, 207, 208, 209, 210, 211, 212, 213, 332, 333, 334, 335, 336, 337, 338, 339, 340, 341, 342, 343, 344, 345,
10) Plumbing	32, 37, 39, 41, 56, 65, 66, 74, 75, 79, 81, 119, 142, 143, 173, 174, 185, 192, 198, 214, 215, 216, 217, 218, 219, 220, 221, 222, 223, 224, 327, 329, 330, 331, 359, 360, 361, 362, 363, 364, 365, 366, 367, 368, 369, 370, 371, 372, 373,

Litigation Strategies "How to Act Professional"

This section is mostly about how to act Professional. But it's also helpful to minimize being sued – this is about adjusting the homeowner's expectations in the beginning.

If you research and investigate all lawsuits involving home inspections, there is one common denominator. You will find that the homeowner did not understand the scope of the home inspection. You will also find is that the client did not have a clear expectation of what he was paying for. It is your job to make it clear from the beginning. Many home buyers think that a home inspection is complete inspection of every square inch which passes or fails the home. This is not the case. Inspectors are not required to identify every minor defect in a home. You should make it clear to your client that you will be reporting on the condition of the home at the *time of the inspection.* In addition, home inspections are to be noninvasive; meaning, if the attic is full of boxes and is inaccessible, you are not required to move any boxes to inspect the area. In addition, if the pilot light is turned off on a piece of equipment, the inspector is not required to turn it on.

One way for an inspector to minimize potential liability is to give the client as much information as possible prior to the home purchase. You should provide useful tips for the homeowner and remind your clients that a home inspection does not reveal every defect that exists and that certain issues are outside the scope of a home inspection. Spend 5-10 min upfront to explain to your client the purpose, requirements, and limitations of a home inspection. Best case scenario would be for the client to join you during the inspection. This is an opportunity to adjust his expectations and get him involved in the process. Inspectors are only doing a visual field performance evaluation.

It is very important to be consistent and follow the 4 steps of the home inspection process.

1) Pre inspection routine, 2) Opening remarks, 3) Inspection itself, and

4) The closing remarks

You should develop a pre inspection routine. Start out be arriving early to your client's house. Become familiar with its design and the surrounding neighborhood. You should also prepare for the inspection. By arriving early, you show your client that his time is valuable. You need to sell the inspection. That's part of it. Make him feel like he is getting value for his money.

The main purpose of the closing discussion is to summarize the major points of the inspection and to make sure that your client understands those issues. At the end of a home inspection, it is good practice to explain to the homeowner that he is now responsible for maintaining their home. Many home buyers give little thought to home maintenance; and assume their home will always be in the same good condition it was in when they first moved in. To help reduce liability, you should give the client as much information as possible about how to maintain the home and look for issues after the purchase.

An inspector can minimize potential liability and lay the foundation for a successful inspection by giving the client as much information as possible prior to the home purchase. Provide the client with a thorough narrative type of report -- **including digital photos --** that clearly identifies any defects or issues that should be investigated further before he purchases the property. Do not give a checklist! If the client later claims that he would not have bought the property if the inspector had noted a particular defect or concern in his report, the inspector's lawyer wants nothing more than to hand the report to the testifying client and point out where the inspector *did* note the defect or claim. Most lawyers agree that the more digital photos you have, the better your defense. The inspection report that you give to the client should be a narrative type report as opposed to just a checklist. You can use a checklist on your inspection; however, it is in your best interest to rewrite all your findings into a professional report with digital photos.

Another way to minimize potential liability is for the inspector to require the client to read and sign the contract prior to the inspection. A contract signed after the inspection is useless. The contract should make the limited scope of the inspection clear. This is where you explain to you client that you will not be testing for compliance with applicable building codes or for the presence of potential dangers arising from asbestos, lead paint, formaldehyde, molds, soil contamination, or other environmental hazards or violations, etc. This paragraph alone can be invaluable if the customer who signed it asserts a claim against the inspector.

By going through your pre inspection routine, you can explain that you do not perform engineering, architectural, plumbing, or any other job function requiring an occupational license. You only perform inspections within the scope of the basic home inspection.

As a final note, you should appreciate the challenges that confront our expertise on the job. Take pride in the fact that if you don't have the answer at hand, you are, at the very least, resourceful enough to find it. You should also take the regular commitment to expand your reach by seeking out the advice and fellowship of colleagues. Always learn and exert the discipline required to increase your education.

A Final Word:

A word of caution! If you have been out of school for a while or a recent college graduate, do not look through this book end to end or the exam contents because you **WILL** get discouraged! There is enough information in it to discourage anyone, including the brightest inspectors!

Remember, the problems in this book are designed based on playing the percentages – based on the exam breakdown. You must work on problem-solving speed and problem-recognition skills. There will be a time during your preparation in which you will start flipping through the book and want to quit because you think that this is too much to learn in this short period of time. **This is completely normal.** You can't expect to get every question correct. This phenomenon is based on the basic learning curve. At one point the curve plateaus without ever increasing until sometime later down the road. This will seem to happen to you as you begin studying. Realize that everyone needs to study. Do not quit! You don't necessarily need to memorize the problems, but become familiar with the steps it takes to solve different types of problems. **Every time you choose to decide to work through one of the practice problems, you are increasing your chances of success.** That is what the book is all about- maximizing your chances of success. Stick to your game plan and get to work!

Phil Jackson is considered one of the greatest basketball coaches of all time by coaching the Chicago Bills to six consecutive NBA championships. He also has the highest winning percentage of any NBA coach. After winning his sixth NBA title, a reporter asked him how he became so lucky. Phil responded by saying that he doesn't believe in luck. He explained to the reporter, *"When you take care of the little things and pay attention to all the details upfront, luck happens. Luck is what happens when you prepare ahead of time and take care of all the little details in practice, and through the natural laws of cause and effect, things just tend to go your way".*

Luck has always been known as when preparation meets opportunity. If you work hard by studying and take care of the little details, things will go your way during the test - and in life in general. The bottom line is that you **need to practice** in order to develop problem recognition skills. Success is not defined by how well you do as compared to other people; it's defined as how well you do relative to your own potential. Winston Churchill said that success is the ability to go from one failure to the next without loss of enthusiasm. You do not have to be great to start, but you have to start in order to be great.

Develop Problem Recognition Skills:

Everyone has the will to win, but you need to have the will to prepare to win. That's what separates winners from losers. You need to put in the hard work up front and prepare by practicing. Wayne Grezky is considered the greatest hockey player ever. He is the leading point-scorer in NHL history, with more assists than any other player has points, and is the only NHL player to total over 200 points in one season – a feat he accomplished four times. However, he was certainly not the biggest or the strongest, but he is considered the smartest player in the history of the game. His size, strength, and basic athletic abilities were not considered impressive but his intelligence and reading of the game were unrivaled, and he could consistently anticipate where the puck was going to be and execute the right move at the right time.

Many sports writers contributed Grezky's success on natural instinct and being a creative genius. However, Grezky admits it has nothing to do with natural instinct and he is far from being a genius. He says that 9 out of 10 people think he's a genius on the ice but says that it is simply not true. He said it has everything to do with how much his dad made him practice as a child and his study of the game. He learned to skate when he was 3 years old and through many hours of practice, he was able to develop a deep understanding of the game's shifting patterns and dynamics. He practiced his entire life until he learned to instantly recognize and capitalize upon emerging patterns of play. On the ice, he never went to where the puck was, but to where the puck was going. He is famous for saying *"that in my own way I've put in almost as much time studying hockey as a medical student puts in studying medicine".*

The bottom line is that you need to practice. **By practicing, you develop problem recognition skills.** This is the key to scoring high. The only way to do this is to solve as many practice problems as you can. Practice is very much underrated and is a lost art these days. However, don't just practice, practice the right things, and you will do the right things on the test. Perfect practice makes perfect. Many people mistakenly attribute genius qualities when what they are witnessing is just a result of practice. A recent student showed that if a person spends 20,000 hours practicing a single task, they become an expert. As soon as you realize that your score has nothing to do with intelligence and luck, instead; has to do with how well you prepare beforehand, you will be on your way to a high score.

Don't Waste Time on Hard Problems:

Many students do not get their best possible score because they waste precious time on hard questions. They simply just run out of time and do not get a chance to answer the easy and medium questions that remained. Time management plays an important factor during the test. You don't need to answer all of the questions right to do well. You only need to answer about 65% of the questions right in order to pass! So if you know you aren't going to be able to finish the exam, you can actually focus on just about 65 percent of the questions, and if you get a good amount of them right (and make sure you still use the last few minutes to guess on the rest) you will pass.

Students often tell us that there just wasn't enough time to finish the test, and we always tell them, **"It is supposed to be that way!"** It's completely normal. The Exam is designed to be hard and not being able to finish. Do not panic.

Don't Let Them in Your Head:

Like most test, they intentionally contain questions that the test developers know will take a lot of time to answer. Don't fall into their traps. Skip the really tough ones, and if you have time, come back to them, or just guess when you are using your last minute or two to fill in all of the questions. Every test has questions that are not only difficult, but also take a lot of time to answer. **They are testing whether you are smart enough to skip these questions.** Many students do not skip hard questions, but instead, waste quality time and still end up getting it wrong.

Using the 80/20 principle as a tool allows you to spend the most amount of time on the problems that matter - **the easy and medium questions.** We handpicked all of the example problems in this book based on the 80/20 rule – all of which have a high percentage chance of showing up on the exam.   In order to maximize your score, you have to search out and find the easy and medium questions and answer those first. Find the "low hanging fruit" type questions first.

Remember, we are trying to play percentages here. You are not only competing against yourself, you are also competing against all the other test takers on test day. **On test day, let all the other test takers waste time trying to solve all the hard problems in sequential order** while you stick to your strategy. There are only 2 things that you have control over on this test: 1) How much time you allot to each question, and 2) How you prepare and practice ahead of time. You must manage your time effectively by following the strategies in this book. You will maximize your score by focusing on about 65% of the test questions and answering correctly than attempting to solve every question in the section perfectly.

The Law of Averages:

(How to Get the Law of Averages to Work for You)

This is a Jim Rohn classic. It gives you a great illustration on how life works and what you can expect. There's actually a bible story called the Parable of the Sower that explains this concept. Success is just a few basic fundamentals practiced every day. Success is also just a numbers game.

If you do something often enough, a ratio will appear. In baseball, we call it batting average. Ask anyone in Sales, and they will tell you the fastest way to get more sales is to get more rejections. It's a rejection game, not a sales game. The more No's you can gather up, the more Yes's you will get. To double your success rate, double your failure rate. Of course, you can improve your skill too and your ratios will improve. But here's what you can do:

You can make up in numbers what you lack in skill.

Even if you can only make 1 sale per every 10 calls (10% closing rate), you can still beat someone who can make 7 sales per 10 calls (70% closing rate). But how? Just by working harder! In a one-month long contest, the better skilled person makes 10 calls and gets his 7 sales, but you make 100 calls and get your 10 sales. 10 beats 7 and you win! You had the same closing ratio of 10%, but you just worked harder than he did by making more calls. Combined with better skills, imagine what you could accomplish! No one said you can only call 10 people. There's no limit on the upper bound.

Success is a numbers game. If you are not good at something, practice it. If you bat 3 out of 10 in major league baseball, you earn $10 million dollars per year. Which means, if you fail 7 times out of 10, still get $10 million per year. You don't have to bat 1000. You don't have to be 100% every single time. Life isn't a "All or Nothing scenario" that you were led to believe in school. In life, you only have to be right one time. You can fail at 6 businesses, but you only need to find one that works. You don't have to bat 1000 to make good money. It's not like in school taking a test where you just have one shot at a good grade. It's not so binary. In life, you can have multiple shots, and you get to choose which pitches to swing at, and you only just need to make one of them to be a success. Also, in life, you are the player, the umpire, the coach, the judge, and the teacher, how can you possibly fail?

In order to win the battle in your own mind, you must trust the law of averages and circumstances will work in your favor and that your life changing efforts will be rewarded. It teaches you that sometimes, you just lose. For no apparent reason you will lose sometimes. It's part of life. Don't ask me why. It's just the way it is. The beautiful part of it is that once you know how it works, you can use it for your advantage! Just keep on going. In life, you will fail more times then you will succeed. Just keep on going. Never stop. I know that if I fail more times than my competitor, I will win in the long game.

The Self-Image:

This concept is the best thing I have ever learned. It's worth the price of this book. It's pure gold. I accidently discovered a book that was written in 1937, called <u>Psycho Cybernetics</u>, written by Dr. Maxwell Maltz, that I believe explains the secret becoming very successful. It changed my life. The book discusses the concept of the Self-Image. Dr. Maltz said that this concept was the greatest discovery in the last century.

Our self-image controls our behavior like a thermostat. The picture you have in your mind is the goal your behavior is programmed to maintain. It can never deviate from this image. **Long term results are always, ALWAYS equal to your self-image.** Your success will never be greater than the image you have of yourself. You can never be more than the picture you have of yourself. Period.

How do you see yourself this summer at the beach? Slim, toned, ripped? Well, no amount of exercise will help you if you <u>can't see it</u>. You might slim up, but you will fall right back to where you started because your self-image is still the same. It will always self-regulate and return to your true self-image. Same with your money blueprint. You will never make more than the money image you have of yourself. Go look up the Secrets of the Millionaire Mind.

Can you see yourself passing this exam? If you can't see it – in your mind's eye- it can never happen. Do you see yourself as a great test taker? Or do you believe that you are a poor test taker? This is why I said to hang up a blank certificate frame earlier. It's the first step to changing your self-image.

What is your Current Self-Image?

The self-image of yourself was developed over years and years of your life and reinforced by your habits every day. You will NEVER become "a great test taker" unless you change your self-image. You need to change the paradigm. You must understand that your self-image is not yours. Your thoughts are not yours either. They are created by your old habits, trying to correct the deviation from your self-image. Our self-image was programmed into us when we were children by your parents and teachers.

By learning how to alter your Self-Image, you never have to be the same person again, only by choice. You will be able to become whoever you want to become. You are limitless. The concept of the self-image is extremely powerful. You can read more about it for yourself. I'm just here to present it. Do your own research.

How to Change Your Self-Image:

The trick is to remake your hidden self-image for success or anything that you want to work on. You CAN learn how to alter it. By changing your self-image, you will discover deep reservoirs of talent and ability within yourself. I overcame my fear of public speaking using this method and many other things.

You need to learn how to do self-image visual exercises. There's also a Goal Card Method involves writing your major goal on a card that you can carry loose in your pocket and reading that as many times as possible during the day. Declarations and Affirmations make a powerful paradigm shifts in your life as well as visual boards. Sounds like bullsh$t, I know, but it isn't.

When you visualize something, you are literally creating a new neural network or pattern within your brain that corresponds to what it is you want to achieve. When you practice creative visualization, you are literally wearing grooves in your mind. Use it to picture the way you would like to feel and act. When you think in different ways than you typically think, and entertain new possibilities, you create the what – if possibility. You'll find yourself just taking action.

Check out a book called "With Winning in Mind", written by Lanny Bassham, He's an Olympian rifle shooter and uses this technique in train other Olympians. Trust me. This isn't bullsh$t guys. It absolutely works. It's the single best thing I ever learned. Ever heard of the Law of attraction? Well, it's real and it's based on Psycho Cybernetics.

State Management:

In the movie Gladiator, right before the one of the battles, he bends down to scoop the sand & dirt with his hands and rubs it between his fingers. That is State Management. He is doing that to mentally prepare for war and to get into battle mode. He is picking up the sand to trigger the State that he wants to be in. Most people are horrible at managing their State. **Life is really all about having the right mindset.** Managing your internal state is so crucial. Get into the right state, and the right behaviors will pour forth automatically. State Management is so critical.

You might be the best test taker in the world, but how do you feel RIGHT NOW before the test? Do you feel nervous? Anxious? Are you focusing on the fight that you had with your wife last night over dirty laundry or how the bank made a mistake on your online account? Or, do you feel clear, confident, and certain? You attract the things in life that you focus on. There are certain ways that we hold our body that can instantly put you into a more positive and empowered state. If your physiology is wrong, it will be difficulty if not impossible to pop into a great state. Make sure it supports the trigger of a peak and empowered state. To get into the correct state, you will learn how to fire off a trigger.

Anchoring:

This comes from a body of psychology called NLP. It deals with how people make change in their lives and how to make sure those changes last. And whenever you use it correctly, it can be an incredible potent tool to have. Let me teach you how to manage your state through anchoring. You can fire off the anchor right before your test to get you in the correct state. Anchoring locks in a very specific state that you want to be able to trigger off at will.

You first need to set an anchor for yourself. Try to remember a time when you accomplished something really spectacular. Bring back those feelings. Were you excited, proud, full of joy? Now hold that feeling, really feel it, let it pour through you, and anchor it to a physical movement – I like to raise my arms in victory. Choose whatever you want.

Now, when you want that same feeling to come back, fire off that same anchor. The same feelings should come back. This is how actors get into character right before the big shoot. Also, how do you think someone like Tony Robbins prepares to go onstage? Do you think he just walks out there and starts talking? No, he pumps himself up by firing off an anchor to get into that high energy state. There's no other way. He knows that he must come on stage in a higher state of energy than the audience- in order for the Law of Transference to work. They will feel what he feels. He knows that they aren't buying his product, they are buying his energy.

Go research on YouTube "Wolf of Wall Street Movie Clip-The money Chant" This is the scene with Matthew McConaughey. In real life, that was his unique way to get into character before filming a crucial scene. But the directors loved it so much, they decided to keep it in the actual movie. You need to find your unique way to get fired up.

Second Effort:

This is a concept that Vince Lombardi, former football coach of the Green Bay Packers football team, taught his players. There are usually only about 168 plays in a typical football game. But only 3-4 plays actually determine the outcome of the game. Since you have no idea when those 3-4 plays are coming up, you must give each play 100% effort! By doing this, you'll be guaranteed to take advantage of maximizing every play. This goes back to the Law of Averages.

Razor's Edge:

Here is a concept taught by Bob Proctor. The line which separates winning from losing is as fine as a razor's edge. The real winners in life are, more often than not, only two or three percent more effective than those who lose.

You need to understand that you can be every bit as effective as anyone you read about or even hear about. The Razor's Edge is simply doing a little bit more … a little bit more than others … a little bit more than is expected … and a little bit more than is necessary. And it doesn't really take any special skills or talents to do it. The good news is you can have the Razor's Edge working for you. It can totally change your life. It did for me.

Now, just consider the tremendous difference you could create in your own life if you were to adopt a similar mental attitude. For example, if you are a person who is working in sales and currently selling only three units a week, what would the consequences be for you if you were to decide to make one additional sale per week, through a conscientious application of the second effort concept? Well, on a weekly basis, it might not appear to be a major breakthrough. However, viewed over the time frame of an entire career, it would actually amount to well over two thousand extra sales. Moreover, from a monetary standpoint, it would mean you would actually receive an extra ten years' income over the span of a forty-year career. Yes, that one sale would be the Razor's Edge difference, which could catapult you into "the big leagues" in your chosen career.

I see it every time in pro sports. The "greatest" golfers ... like Tiger Woods ... are only 3 or 4 strokes better than the "poorest" golfers in the tournament, but their winnings are dozens of times higher than those who come in second, third, or fourth place. Running backs fall forward to pick up a few extra yards each play. What does that do over the course of a game, a season, a career...

How can you get the Razor's Edge working for you?

1) Refuse to Settle for the Basics:

For example, you may have mastered the basics of reading by the fifth or sixth grade. But have you done anything since then to improve your reading skills? And you may have mastered the basics of arithmetic, but have you gone beyond that to master the skills required for saving, investing, and budgeting for your future?

2) Decide to become an expert in Something:

Once people understand the basics of something, they usually stop their learning in that area. Only a small percentage of people ever go on to become the acknowledged experts in a particular area. And they are the ones, of course, who typically receive the largest incomes. That's why you should look at what you're doing and ask yourself, "How good am I at doing it?" and "How much better could I be?"

3) Dedicate Your Time to Study:

All you have to do is study one hour a day in your chosen field, and in five years you will be an expert in that field. In Proctor's words, "If you were to follow this schedule rigorously, in a relatively short span of time you would stand among your peers like a giraffe in a herd of field mice."

4) Turn Your Car into A Library:

Turn your radio off and your CD player or iPhone on. If you drive thousands of miles to work or errands each year, then listen to educational, motivational CDs. You can learn basically just about anything. Make recordings of your Control Sheet I discussed earlier.

5) Add the Razor's Edge Element to Your Job:

Perhaps you're in a customer service position. You will be astounded at what happens if you change your attitude towards your customers. If you tend to see customers as an interruption OF your business ... instead the reason FOR your business ... you're bound to lose some customers. But if you think of ways to sharpen your customer service skills ... and then actually do it ... you'll see an amazing difference in how you feel and in how much they buy. Try smiling at every customer. Give everyone a genuine, welcoming "hello" instead of perfunctory "hi." And make sure you go out of your way to thank them for their business.

Before a work meeting, really prepare for it- strive to be the most prepared person in the room, read all the emails, the manuals, etc.. take notes. You will be seen as the smartest in the room – just by simply preparing for the meeting! Most people don't even bother to read the manual. This takes no extra skill.

You are only one inch ... one step ... one idea ... away from turning onto the boulevard of beauty in your own life... and the inches are everywhere.

How to get this to work for you:

Do one extra problem a day, it will add up over time. Does that take any special skill? No. Did most test takers do this too? No. But why? Because it's easy Not to Do. What's easy... is also easy not to do.

Learning Curve:

There will be a time during your preparation in which you will start flipping through the *this book* and want to quit because you think that this is too much to learn in this short period of time. **This is completely normal.** You can't expect to get every question correct. This phenomenon is based on the basic learning curve. At one point, the curve plateaus without ever increasing until sometime later down the road. This will seem to happen to you as you begin studying. Realize that everyone needs to study. Do not quit! Don't judge your progress by how many questions you are getting correct in practice. Don't fall into the trap of thinking that you should be getting 60% of all the practice questions right if you want to pass the actual exam.

Don't pressure yourself for perfection, keep it all in perspective. In basketball, you have to shoot 50% to be considered an average player. If you make an extra 10 shots per hundred, you are an All-Star. In real life, the odds are a little different. You don't have to be right every time. In fact, it doesn't matter how many times you strike out or fail a test. In life, to be a success, you only have to be right once. It doesn't matter how many problems you get wrong in practice; it only matters that get a percentage of the problems correct during the actual exam, and that percentage changes for each exam.

Expect to Struggle:

You should expect to struggle while first starting to work problems in this book. It's normal. You are clearing out the cobwebs, , and brushing up on material you learned before. If you aren't getting problems wrong and doing stupid mistakes with units then something is definitely wrong. You aren't trying hard enough to succeed. Don't be afraid to fail.

Examples of great men and women failing have become emblematic of success: Michael Jordan, the greatest basketball player in the history of the game (sorry Kobe) missed over 9,000 shots in his career and he lost almost 300 games. 26 times he's been trusted to take the game-winning shot and missed. He failed over and over and over again in his life. And that is why he succeeded. Babe Ruth struck out 1,335 times to get his near record 714 home runs. Thomas Edison persisted through 1,300 failed experiments until he finally invented the light bulb. Abraham Lincoln lost over 90% of the debates his participated in but he is still considered the best debater of any president. If you read the biography of any famous actor, you will learn that they did not get the role more often than they did land the role. The best comedians of all time; Richard Prior, Steve Kinison, bombed on stage more often, at least in the beginning, than they killed it. True victory is preceded by defeat.

Only Have to be Right One Time:

Doesn't matter how many times you failed before. You only have to be right one time. If you focus, visualize your goal, and avoid the naysayers, success will come. Progress is never in a straight line. It will have dips. Your criteria for success should be you taking action, not solving practice problems correctly. As you work through your mistakes, it is like swinging a machete through a thick vegetated forest. You are creating new pathways that didn't exist before. As you study, you are forcing yourself to learn new skills by creating new pathways and connections. Once you create the new pathway, it's always there and it cannot be erased. Everyone has a failure curve. But the trick is to exhaust your failure curve during practice (by working as many practice problems as you can) not waiting during the actual exam. In sales, if you want to double your income, you need to double your rejections. It's a numbers game.

Avoid the Naysayers:

Avoid discussing the exam with other people while waiting in line before the exam or even before the exam. There will be some groups of people (I call them the HERD) who say that "this exam is stupid and a waste of time", "it doesn't make you a better home inspector", "in the old days they used to just hand these out when you graduated", "you can't make any money as a PE anyway", "bla bla bla" etc. You want to avoid the naysayers and all that negative energy all together.

It's best to try to relax while you are waiting in line for the exam center to open its doors and not get caught up in meaningless discussions about the exam or people's opinions. Stay cool, calm, collected, visualize your goal and stay positive. Use this time to take pride in the fact that you prepared and feel confident about the exam and look forward to the challenge.

Also don't make these grand announcements on social media about taking the exam. If you fail, you will have to relive it all over again when everyone asks if you passed.

Don't be Afraid to Fail:

Don't be afraid to fail. When you tell yourself you are too tired or don't have time to study, realize that someone else out there is working hard and getting stronger at working these problems. Mike Tyson used to wake up to jog at 3 am in the morning when preparing for a boxing match. A reporter once asked him why? Mike simply responded, *"because I know that my opponent isn't"*. Remember that you are also going up against other test takers the same day. You don't have to get all the problems correct; you just have to be better than about 35 % of all the other test takers. Visualize your goal and stay focused on working the practice problems in this book. Gain every advantage you can over other test takers. Study a little bit each day. Work 1 or 2 problems in the morning, a few at lunch time, and max it out at night. When you start gaining momentum by studying a little bit each day, a compounding effect starts happening. Since compounding is an exponential function, it will seem to get easier and you will be amazed by how much material you have gone through. Even on days when you are the most tired and don't feel like studying, try to do just one thing to improve yourself by 1%. Improving yourself by just 1% per day for one month is not 30% better... it is much more than that because of the compounding effect. I secret I learned long ago is that **you can make up in numbers what you lack in skill**. Just put in more study time than the rest of the test takers – and you will succeed. You don't have to be some genius home inspector, just put in more time practicing the test questions.

I truly believe that we are all so much more capable than what we were led to believe throughout our lives and especially in school. Most people only use a fraction, maybe 5 or 10%, of their potential. It's time to tap into the other 95%. Whether or not you choose to find the time to study is entirely up to you.

Hard Work:

If you want to go through life trying to make other people happy and not taking any risks, then ignore all the advice in this book. But if you want to win, there is no getting around hard, hard work. You should be hungry to make your mark on this world and willing to work towards your goals. The best investment you can make is in yourself. Remember, you are the average of the top 5 people that you hang around. Who are you hanging around with? Where will these people be in 5 years? Are they pushing themselves to be better professionally?

The fact that you invested in this book and are trying to reach your goal, means that you are already 10 times more likely to pass this exam than the average test taker. Remember, every time you work through one of the practice problems in this book or flip through this book, you are **increasing your chances of passing**. If you prepare using this book and understand and practice all of the questions, you will pass on your first try.

Outcome Independence:

Let go of the outcome. The best coaches do not focus on winning; they focus on systems and processes. You can't control the other team and there are too many variables. It's important to only focus on what you need to do next, and doing it to the best of your ability. The process is really what you have to do day in and day out to be successful. Nick Saban talks about processes all the time. Instead of asking their players to focus on winning the championship or the next big game, the best coaches ask them to focus on what the next action is. The next drill. The next play. The next touchdown. It's not the outcome that's important, but the process.

Stop worrying about if you will pass or fail this exam, just focus on what your next step is…. Did you work any practice problems today? Are you learning the format and layout of this book? Do you know how long you have to solve each problem? Did you work and problems during lunchtime today or did you just surf the web for 45 minutes? Focus on things that you can control.

Eliminate the clutter and all the things that are going on outside and focus on the things that you can control with how you sort of go about and take care of your business. That's something that's ongoing, and it can never change. It's the journey that's important. You can't worry about end results. It's about what you control, every minute of every day. You always must have a winning attitude and discipline, in practices, weight training, conditioning, in the classroom, in everything. It's a process. When you commit to a process over an outcome, you redirect your focus on what is within your inner locus of control; discipline, motivation and organization to name a few, drive the actions needed to necessitate the outcome you're moving towards.

When you're committed to the process, you always win because you're improving daily. You're constantly moving towards what you want because of the tiny actions you're taking. Remember, your criteria for success is taking action each day. You must design and commit to a system for change; an efficient process where positive outcomes are an inevitable outcome. Ask yourself: "What could I do daily that would guarantee extraordinary result results?

A Final Word:

A word of caution! If you have been out of school for a while or a recent college graduate, do not look through this book end to end or the exam contents because you **WILL** get discouraged! There is enough information in it to discourage anyone, including the brightest inspectors!

Remember, the problems in this book are designed based on playing the percentages – based on the exam breakdown. You must work on problem-solving speed and problem-recognition skills. There will be a time during your preparation in which you will start flipping through the book and want to quit because you think that this is too much to learn in this short period of time. **This is completely normal.** You can't expect to get every question correct. This phenomenon is based on the basic learning curve. At one point the curve plateaus without ever increasing until sometime later down the road. This will seem to happen to you as you begin studying. Realize that everyone needs to study. Do not quit! You don't necessarily need to memorize the problems, but become familiar with the steps it takes to solve different types of problems. **Every time you choose to decide to work through one of the practice problems, you are increasing your chances of success.** That is what the book is all about- maximizing your chances of success. Stick to your game plan and get to work!

Phil Jackson is considered one of the greatest basketball coaches of all time by coaching the Chicago Bills to six consecutive NBA championships. He also has the highest winning percentage of any NBA coach. After winning his sixth NBA title, a reporter asked him how he became so lucky. Phil responded by saying that he doesn't believe in luck. He explained to the reporter, *"When you take care of the little things and pay attention to all the details upfront, luck happens. Luck is what happens when you prepare ahead of time and take care of all the little details in practice, and through the natural laws of cause and effect, things just tend to go your way".*

Luck has always been known as when preparation meets opportunity. If you work hard by studying and take care of the little details, things will go your way during the test - and in life in general. The bottom line is that you **need to practice** in order to develop problem recognition skills. Success is not defined by how well you do as compared to other people; it's defined as how well you do relative to your own potential. Winston Churchill said that success is the ability to go from one failure to the next without loss of enthusiasm. You do not have to be great to start, but you have to start in order to be great.

Good Luck !

Now get to work!

1) Which of the following <u>best</u> describes the statement shown below that appears in a typical home inspection report?

"The water heater is in good condition for its age."

(A) Conclusion

(B) Recommendation

(C) Description

(D) Disclaimer

2) Which of the following conditions would be <u>least</u> critical to your client's safety?

(A) Missing smoke alarms in the house

(B) A non-reversing garage door opener

(C) Missing PT relief valve on the water heater

(D) A pin hole in the heat exchanger

3) It is important to maintain a positive grade away from a structure of at least _____ inch drop per foot for the first six feet.

(A) ¾

(B) 1

(C) ¼

(D) ½

4) The minimum run for a residential stair tread is:

(A) 9 in.

(B) 8 in.

(C) 7 in.

(D) 4 in.

5) Standard three light electrical testers are not 100% reliable because:

(A) Three light testers sometimes have broken wiring

(B) Some receptacles only have two prongs

(C) Different test device manufactures have different light patterns

(D) Three light testers will not detect multiple wiring problems

6) Bulging plaster is observed high up on several bedroom walls. The primary concern is the bulging plaster is a(n):

(A) Installation defect

(B) Indication the home is very old

(C) Indication the air conditioner leaked

(D) Potential safety issue

7) When calculating the cooling loads for an HVAC system, what are the types of heat transfer that must be considered?

(A) Conductive and latent heat

(B) Sensible and latent heat

(C) Sensible and conductive heat

(D) Radiant heat only

8) Which of the following materials would be most likely to have the highest R-value?

(A) 6" fiberglass batt insulation

(B) 12" cast-in-place concrete wall

(C) 2" extruded polystyrene panel

(D) Triple insulated glazing system with ½" air spaces

9) As home inspector, you can often determine the approximate age of a home by observing how it was constructed. Which of the following choices represents the method of construction that is the oldest?

(A) Insulated Concrete Form (ICF) construction

(B) Balloon framing

(C) Platform framing

(D) Post and beam construction

10) Which of the following locations is often prone to a deficiency when inspecting Exterior Insulation and Finishing (EIFS) wall system?

(A) On the inside wall of the home

(B) At the corners of the installation (around windows)

(C) Along the bottom edge

(D) The center of large expanses of EIFS

11) During an inspection, you observe that a heat pump is not working and that the condensate pan under the air handler is full of water. What probably happened?

(A) This must indicate that there is a leak in the heat exchanger and as a safety precaution the unit turned off.

(B) The full condensate pan indicates that the fan in the air handler is not functioning.

(C) Since the pan was full, the condensate overflow switch turned the unit off in order to ensure that condensate did not spill.

(D) The full condensate pan means that the air handler main pinion gear disengaged and turned the unit off.

12) Home inspectors can never be sued because they are protected by the latest codes and jurisdiction.

True or False?

13) Fill in the Blank: The V-3 rule states that a wall can usually be considered unsafe if it leans to such an extent that a plumb line passing through its center of gravity does not fall inside the middle _____ of its base.

(A) One-fourth

(B) One-half

(C) Its base cubed

(D) One-third

14) What is the definition of a Collar beam?

(A) 2000 psi Concrete without reinforcement

(B) 2x4s braced in between each stud.

(C) Nominal 1 or 2-inch-thick members which connect opposite roof rafters

(D) Typically, a 2x6 or greater support in which a ledger beam rests

15) Which of the following is <u>not</u> up to code?

(A) Emergency egress windows and doors should not have bars unless they are releasable from inside without a key, tool, or special knowledge.

(B) Egress windows must have a clear height of at least 16 inches

(C) Every sleeping room and habitable basement room should have at least one operable window or exterior door for emergency egress or rescue.

(D) Egress windows should have a clear minimum opening of 5.7 square feet

16) Which of the following is not normally checked during aluminum siding inspection?

(A) Removing a piece of siding in order to inspect the wood behind it.

(B) Checking for loose or broken pieces

(C) Checking for grounding

(D) Inspecting all caulked joints

17) When inspecting a home, you observe a whitish, cottony growth on the surface of the baseboards. Which of the following types of fungi is most likely the cause?

(A) Brown-rot fungi

(B) Green-rot fungi

(C) White-rot fungi

(D) Black-rot fungi

18) Which should never be included in your report after a pool inspection?

(A) The risk and probability of children falling in the pool

(B) The presence of GFCI devices on pool lights

(C) Pool and deck surface condition

(D) Proximity to electrical wires, location of electrical outlets to the home

19) Which of the following is a benefit or right for which the parties to a contract must bargain?

(A) Contractual amendments

(B) Consideration

(C) Acts of God

(D) Latent defects

20) One who has contracted to be responsible for another or one who assumes responsibilities or debts in the event of default is known as the:

(A) Privity

(B) Home inspector

(C) Client

(D) Surety

21) Which of the following is not a solid fuel heating device?

(A) A coal furnace

(B) An electric heater

(C) A woodstove

(D) A fireplace

22) Is the roofing material on a house considered a part of the roof drainage system?

(A) Yes

(B) No

23) As a home inspector, you are required to observe and/or test all the readily accessible components of each system. Which of the following is not considered to be a readily accessible component of a room?

(A) A receptacle in a closet

(B) The doorknob on the closet door

(C) A small window

(D) Nails or screws in the floor

24) According to the International Residential Code (IRC), rafters are to be fastened to ridge boards or gusset plates if the pitch of the roof is greater than or equal to what angle?

(A) 3/12

(B) 5/12

(C) 4/12

(D) 2/12

25) As an inspector, when you observe a component, you are making this type of examination:

(A) Opinion

(B) Recommendation

(C) Visual

(D) Analyzing

26) How large should the footing or foundation for a masonry fireplace be?

(A) > 12 inches thick and extend 12 inches beyond the fireplace on all sides.

(B) > 12 inches thick and extend 6 inches beyond the fireplace on all sides

(C) > 6 inches thick and extend 12 inches beyond the fireplace on all sides

(D) > 6 inches thick and extend 6 inches beyond the fireplace on all sides

27) As a home inspector, you are required to inspect a "representative number" of electrical outlets in a building. What does this mean?

(A) Testing one electrical outlet in each room of the structure

(B) Randomly inspect electrical outlets in the structure

(C) Selecting only outlets that your client requests

(D) Selecting a percentage of all the electrical outlets in the structure

28) Every habitable room in a residential home should contain this much glazing area?

(A) ≥10% of floor area

(B) ≥15% of floor area

(C) ≥ 2% of floor area

(D) ≥ 8% of floor area

29) Which of the following types of inspections uses measurements, tests, calculations and instruments to gather information on the structure under inspection?

(A) Ball park

(B) Technically exhaustive

(C) Visual

(D) Quality

30) Under what circumstances does the IRC allow builders to add additional loads, such as a water heater, to a wood truss?

(A) If the city engineer says it is okay

(B) If the owner approves it as a contract modification

(C) It is never allowed

(D) Only if a licensed professional engineer has verified it is acceptable

31) The roof drainage system should discharge water how far from the foundation if it does not tie into a drainpipe?

(A) > 2 ft

(B) > 3 ft

(C) > 4 ft

(D) > 5 ft

32) What is the common minimum and maximum pressure for a water supply system in a residential building?

(A) 40 and 80 psi

(B) 30 and 70 psi

(C) 50 and 90 psi

(D) 60 and 80 psi

33) Ground-fault circuit interceptors (GFCI) are required in which of the following locations?

(A) Outdoor outlets

(B) Bathroom outlets

(C) Countertop outlets

(D) All of the above

34) An unvented conditioned attic is permitted only when:

(A) It is never permitted

(B) There is not a vapor retarder applied to the floor of the attic, but there is insulation applied to the underside of the roof deck

(C) There is a not vapor retarder applied on the floor of the attic, but there is an exhaust fan.

(D) There is a vapor retarder applied on the floor of the attic, but there is no insulation applied to the underside of the roof deck

35) Is a "cross connection" is a physical connection between two electrical circuits?

Yes or No?

36) All of the following are considered structural components of a building, except:

(A) Non-load bearing interior wall

(B) The floor of a 2 story building

(C) The floor of the main floor of a 1 story building

(D) An exterior wall.

37) A horizontal drainpipe should have a proper slope, which is?

(A) $\geq 1/8:1$

(B) $\leq 1/2:1$

(C) 1/8:1 to 1/2:1

(D) Slope = 0

38) The waterproof material in a bathroom should extend how far above a showerhead?

(A) $\geq 3"$

(B) $> 3"$

(C) $\geq 4"$

(D) $\geq 5"$

39) An on-site water quality test is generally done only on which of the following structures?

(A) Structures built prior to 1978

(B) Balloon framing structures only

(C) Non-municipal water supply

(D) Municipal water supply

40) All of the following are components of a roof drainage system except?

(A) Gutters

(B) Splash blocks

(C) Downspouts

(D) Shingles

41) What is the maximum allowable distance between cleanouts for drain pipes according to the IRC?

(A) 25 feet horizontally

(B) 50 feet horizontally

(C) 75 feet horizontally

(D) 100 feet horizontally

42) What is the minimum slope requirement of a roof with asphalt shingles?

(A) $\geq 3:12$

(B) $\geq 4:12$

(C) $\geq 2:12$

(D) $\geq 1:12$

43) How far above grade should a concrete slab extend?

(A) At least 5"

(B) At least 8"

(C) At least 6"

(D) At least 3"

44) If your standard reporting form does not include a section for a defect that you observe, you should:

(A) Don't include it on the report

(B) Report the defect verbally and make a note of it on the report

(C) Only include it if your client points it out

(D) Report the defect verbally but do not have to write it down

45) Rusting lintels are found over the top of?

(A) Aluminum sinks

(B) Wood headers

(C) Metal I-beams

(D) Windows

46) Masonry veneer weep holes should be:

(A) Above grade

(B) Below Grade

(C) Filled with flowable cement

(D) Checked by an engineer

47) Which of the following would you most likely to find on a typical GFCI receptacle?

(A) Small batteries

(B) TP relief valves

(C) Test and reset buttons

(D) Dimmer switch

48) Which of the following is correct regarding notching wood joists?

(A) Notching not permitted in middle 1/3 of span.

(B) Notching is never allowed

(C) Notching is allowed if the city inspector doesn't see it

(D) What the client doesn't know want hurt him

49) GFCI circuitry continuously monitors:

(A) Current in the ground and neutral wires to make sure they match.

(B) Voltage in the wires to make sure they match.

(C) Current in the hot and ground wires to make sure they match.

(D) Current in the hot and neutral wires to make sure they match.

50) What is the term used to describe when 2 black wires are connected to a single fuse?

(A) Double tip

(B) Double circuits

(C) Double tap

(D) Double trouble

51) How many years must home inspection records be kept by the home inspector?

(A) 1 year

(B) 2 years

(C) 3 years

(D) 4 years

52) Porches, balconies, or raised floors more than 30 inches above grade shall have a guardrail not less than how many inches?

(A) 36 inches

(B) 42 inches

(C) 12 inches

(D) 30 inches

53) A main electrical service entrance is routed over a flat roof. If the homeowner decides to build a deck over the roof area, what is the required clearance?

(A) 15 feet

(B) 10 feet

(C) 8 feet

(D) 12 feet

54) A home inspector is required to move the floor insulation behind an earth filled porch and at plumbing locations:

True or False?

55) In the heating cycle for a heat pump, the inside coil functions as a:

(A) Heat exchanger

(B) Condenser

(C) Back flow preventer

(D) Evaporator

56) In a hydronic heating system, the role of the expansion tank is to

(A) Allow for expansion of water

(B) Keep the system pressurized

(C) Keep the PT relief valve from malfunctioning

(D) Remove excessive vapor pressure from the water

57) Which of the following is an opening in a wall or parapet that allows water to drain from the   roof?

(A) A weep hole

(B) A scupper

(C) A squirrel hole

(D) A tile drain

58) The fibers in the lower section of a simply supported beam are in:

(A) Compression

(B) Torsion

(C) Shear

(D) Tension

59) A manufactured roof truss transfers or applies which of the following loading to the walls of the home?

(A) Horizontal

(B) Intermittent

(C) Axial

(D) Vertical

60) If a person violates the provision of the Administrative Code they can be found guilty of:

(A) Class 2 Misdemeanor

(B) Class 3 Felony

(C) Simple misdemeanor

(D) Class 1 Misdemeanor

61) When the refrigerate leaves the AC compressor it is:

(A) Cold pressure liquid

(B) Hot high pressure gas

(C) Hot low pressure gas

(D) Cold high pressure gas

62) Which is the following is the most common and most destructive wood- destroying insect?

(A) Termites

(B) Beetles

(C) Carpenter Bees

(D) Carpenter Ants

63) A home inspection is supposed to be:

(A) Visual inspection only

(B) Technically accurate with field measurements

(C) Visual and non-invasive

(D) Made public knowledge

64) Which of the following is a crystalline deposit on surfaces of masonry, stucco or concrete and has a whitish appearance?

(A) Toxic bacteria

(B) White algae

(C) Salt

(D) Efflorescence

65) You are inspecting a flat where and observe ponding water in an area of 20'x10' and is 1" deep. Estimate the additional load on the roof due to the ponding water.

(A) 2,080 pounds

(B) 1,040 pounds

(C) 540 pounds

(D) 80 pounds

66) Which of the following plumbing traps are not allowed and sometimes illegal?

(A) Z

(B) P

(C) S

(D) U

67) What is the purpose of a plumbing trap?

(A) To allow all water to drain after the fixture's use to create a seal

(B) To retain a small amount of pressure after the fixture's use to create a vacuum

(C) To retain a small amount of water vapor after the fixture's use to create a siphoning affect

(D) To retain a small amount of water after the fixture's use to create a seal

Exam # 1 Solutions:

<u>Solution to Question # 1:</u>

(A) Conclusion.

<u>Solution to Question # 2:</u>

(D) A pin hole in the heat exchanger.

Pin holes may be small leaks that scab over with rust scale intermittently and they usually mean that the heat exchanger is near the end of its life. Answers choices A, B, C, are safety hazards that need <u>immediate attention</u>.

<u>Solution to Question # 3:</u>

(B). 1.

Improper grading which doesn't correctly slope away from the foundation can allow excessive amounts of groundwater to collect in the soil around basement walls.

<u>Solution to Question # 4:</u>

(A). 9"

Max. rise is 7-3/4"

<u>Solution to Question # 5:</u>

(D). Three light testers will not detect multiple wiring problems.

Simple three light testers cannot detect two potentially serious house wiring errors: (1) neutral and ground reversed at the receptacle. (2) a "bootleg" ground, where the neutral and ground pins have been connected together at the receptacle.

<u>Solution to Question # 6:</u>

(D) Potential safety issue.

Bulging, loose, or missing plaster is usually considered a cosmetic issue; however, it is a safety issue because it is heavy and can hurt someone if it falls below.

Solution to Question # 7:

(B). Sensible and latent heat.

Sensible heat is energy that causes a change in temperature. Latent heat is energy that comes from matter changing its state, but not its temperature. HVAC systems must deal with both of these types of heat loads in order to make the indoor environment comfortable. The terms "radiant" and "conductive" refer to types of heat transfer but not to an actual value of heat gain or loss.

Solution to Question # 8:

(A) 6" fiberglass batt insulation.

You do not necessarily need to memorize all the values, but instead, try to reason this question out. Fiberglass batt insulation contains many tiny air pockets, which help to increase its R-value. A 12" concrete wall has very little air in it, therefore, resulting in a low R-value. Six inches of fiberglass batt insulation could be expected to have an R-value of around 18.

Solution to Question # 9

(D) Post and beam construction.

Post and beam construction was used in 1700. Balloon framing started to be used in the 1800s. Platform framing became popular in the middle of the 20th century. ICFs, began to be used in the late 1960s and 1970s.

Solution to Question # 10:

(B). At the corners of the installation (around windows).

Corners have a greater potential for leakage. The corner of the jamb and the sill is especially prone to leakage, because water can get in the jamb and then run down the edge and back into the wall at the corner.

Solution to Question # 11:

(C) Since the pan was full, the condensate overflow switch turned the unit off in order to ensure that condensate did not spill.

Some units have a condensate overflow switch that will turn the unit off so that the condensate does not spill out of the pan. To fix the problem, just empty out the pan. The other answers would not stop the unit from functioning immediately.

Solution to Question # 12:

False.

Solution to Question # 13:

(D) One-third.

If the line does not lie within the center one third of the wall, the wall is unstable. If there are joists resting on the wall, even less lean is allowed before the wall is unstable.

Solution to Question # 14:

(C) Nominal 1 or 2 inch thick members which connect opposite roof rafters.

Collar beams serve to stiffen the roof structure

Solution to Question # 15:

(B) Egress windows must have a clear height of at least 16 inches.

The window must have: A minimum clear opening width must be at least 20". A minimum clear opening height must be at least 36". A minimum clear opening size must be at least 5.7 square feet.

Solution to Question # 16:

(A) Inspect the wood behind the siding by removing a piece.

A general home inspection is a non-invasive, visual examination of the accessible areas.

Solution to Question # 17:

(C) White-rot fungi.

White-rot fungi break down the lignin in wood, leaving the lighter-colored cellulose behind.

Solution to Question # 18:

(A) The risk and probability of children falling in the pool.

You should never make future predications, just simply report of your observations at the time of the inspection.

Solution to Question # 19:

(B) Consideration.

Consideration can take many forms, primarily money, but can also include time, conversion, or forbearance.

Solution to Question # 20:

(D) Surety.

Also known as a "guarantor"

Solution to Question # 21:

(B) An electric heater.

Solution to Question # 22:

(B) No.

Solution to Question # 23:

(D) Nails or screws in the floor.

This will be considered concealed since you would have to remove them.

Solution to Question # 24:

(A) 3/12.

Solution to Question # 25:

(C) Visual.

Solution to Question # 26:

(B) > 12 inches thick and extend six inches beyond the fireplace on all sides.

Solution to Question # 27:

(A) Testing one electrical outlet in each room of the structure.

Solution to Question # 28:

(D) ≥ 8% of floor area.

Solution to Question # 29:

(B) Technically exhaustive

Solution to Question # 30:

(D) Only if a licensed professional engineer has verified it is acceptable.

Solution to Question # 31:

(D) > 5 ft.

Solution to Question # 32:

(A) 40 and 80 psi.

Solution to Question # 33:

(D) All of the above.

Solution to Question # 34:

(B) There is not a vapor retarder applied to the floor of the attic, but there is insulation applied to the underside of the roof deck.

Solution to Question # 35:

No.

Solution to Question # 36:

(A) Non-load bearing interior wall.

Solution to Question # 37:

(C) 1/8:1 to 1/2:1

Solution to Question # 38:

(A) ≥ 3"

Solution to Question # 39:

(C) Non-municipal water supply.

Solution to Question # 40:

(D) Shingles.

Roofing material is not considered part of the roof drainage system.

Solution to Question # 41:

(D) 100 feet horizontally.

The International Residential Code requires cleanouts for drainpipes to be established at intervals throughout the drain system.

Solution to Question # 42:

(C) ≥ 2:12

Solution to Question # 43:

(B) At least 6"

Solution to Question # 44:

(B) Report the defect verbally and make a note of it on the report.

Always make a note of every deficiency on your written report.

Solution to Question # 45:

(D) Windows.

Solution to Question # 46:

(A) Above grade.

Solution to Question # 47:

(C) Test and reset buttons.

Solution to Question # 48:

(A) Notching not permitted in middle 1/3 of span.

Solution to Question # 49:

(D) Current in the hot and neutral wires to make sure they match.

Solution to Question # 50:

(C) Double tap.

Solution to Question # 51:

(C) 3 years.

Solution to Question # 52:

(A) 36 inches.

Solution to Question # 53:

(B) 10 feet.

Solution to Question # 54:

True.

Solution to Question # 55:

(B) Condenser.

Solution to Question # 56:

(A) Allow for expansion of water.

Solution to Question # 57:

(B) A scupper.

Solution to Question # 58:

(D) Tension.

The top fibers are in compression since they are being squeezed, the bottom fibers would be in tension since they are being stretched.

Solution to Question # 59:

(D) Vertical.

Solution to Question # 60:

(A) Class 2 Misdemeanor.

Solution to Question # 61:

(B) Hot high pressure gas.

Solution to Question # 62:

(A) Termites

Carpenter ant damage is generally more localized than damage caused by termite infestation. Older homes are generally more likely to experience beetle infestation. This bee is primarily a nuisance pest, but if allowed to reinfest the same areas, structural damage could occur.

Solution to Question # 63:

(C) Visual and non-invasive.

Solution to Question # 64:

(D) Efflorescence.

Solution to Question # 65:

(B) 1,040 pounds.

To quickly estimate this kind of questions, water weights about 5 pounds for every inch deep for every square foot. In the example, 20' x 10' = 200 square feet, therefore, 200 x 5 = 1000 pounds.

Solution to Question # 66:

(C) S

S-traps tend to easily siphon dry even when well-vented.

Solution to Question # 67:

(D) To retain a small amount of water after the fixture's use to create a seal.

This prevents sewer gas from passing from the drain pipes back into the occupied space of the building

68) Gold deck screws are designed to resist:

(A) Shear

(B) Torsion

(C) Compression

(D) Withdrawal

69) Fasteners designed to resist withdrawal, such as deck screws, are weak in:

(A) Tension resistance

(B) Shear resistance

(C) Compression resistance

(D) Strain

70) All of the following are advantages of aluminum siding, except:

(A) It is waterproof

(B) It is dent resistant

(C) It is fireproof

(D) It is recyclable

71) You are inspecting aluminum siding and observe that it has been installed in contact with the ground and has a slight outward bulging at the bottom. This can be an indication of which of the following?

(A) The building sills and/or lower walls have been damaged by the grounding bar

(B) The building sills and/or lower walls have been recently repaired

(C) The building sills and/or lower walls have been damaged by rot or pests

(D) There was a manufacturing error

72) What is the purpose of an anti-scold valve?

(A) To mix hot water in with incoming cold water

(B) To prevent backflow

(C) Assist the PT valve on a water heater

(D) To mix cold water in with outgoing hot water

73) Installation of anti-scald valves is typically:

(A) Simple and inexpensive

(B) Complex but inexpensive

(C) Simple and expensive

(D) Complex and inexpensive

74) Why is <u>backflow</u> is a potential problem in a water system?

(A) It can spread contaminated water back through a distribution system.

(B) It can reduce pressure to your distribution system

(C) It can spread toxic fumes into the home's ventilation system.

(D) It can cause carbon monoxide poisoning

75) What is designed to prevent the reverse flow of water in a potable water system?

(A) Back trap preventer

(B) Back switch preventer

(C) Back-pressure preventer

(D) Backflow preventer

76) During an inspection you observe aluminum wiring, which of the following should you report to your client?

(A) Since aluminum wiring is a safety hazard, recommend that your client not buy the house.

(B) The wiring should be evaluated by a qualified electrician

(C) Call you friend who is an electrical contractor to come give a recommendation

(D) Recommend that all of the wiring has to be replaced

77) Which of the following is a colorless, odorless, poisonous gas that forms from incomplete combustion of fuels, such as natural or liquefied petroleum gas, oil, wood or coal?

(A) Carbon dioxide

(B) Carbon fibers

(C) Nitrous oxide

(D) Carbon monoxide

78) High concentrations of carbon monoxide can kill in less than:

(A) 30 minutes

(B) 8 hours

(C) 5 min

(D) 5 seconds

79) Which of the following is the reverse from normal flow direction within a piping system as the result of the downstream pressure being higher than the supply pressure?

(A) Back-siphonage

(B) Back-pressure

(C) Front-pressure

(D) Back-flow

80) All of the following should be components of a home inspection, except?

(A) Recommendations

(B) The reason why certain things were not inspected

(C) A structural analysis of the framing

(D) Deficiency implications

81) Which of the following is the reverse from normal flow direction within a piping system that is caused by negative pressure in the supply piping?

(A) Front-suctioning

(B) Front-siphonage

(C) Back-suctioning

(D) Back-siphonage

82) Home inspectors are required to report on compliance with code regulations?

True or False?

83) Which of the following represents the average duration of a typical home inspection?

(A) 2 ½ hours

(B) 30 minutes

(C) 4 ½ hours

(D) 2 days

84) Which of the following statements is true?

(A) A home inspector is required to climb on a roof

(B) A home inspector is not required to report causes of conditions

(C) A home inspector is required to give a warranty or guarantee

(D) A home inspector is required to turn on and operate systems that are shut down

85) As an inspector, you have an obligation to all the following people, except?

(A) The buyer

(B) Yourself

(C) The listing agent

(D) Your friend who is a general contractor

86) The purpose of a home inspection is to determine the fair market value of the home.

True or False?

87) What is one of the top reasons that you would like to have your client be present during the inspection?

(A) To be able to recommend potential work for your friend who is an electrician

(B) To reduce liability

(C) So you try to upsell a separate inspection, such as a swimming pool inspection

(D) So you don't have to write a report later on, you can give him your checklist.

88) A home inspection should be consisted of how many parts?

(A) 1: The inspection itself

(B) 2: Pre inspection routine and then the inspection itself

(C) 3: Inspection and the closing remarks

(D) 4: Pre inspection routine, opening remarks, inspection itself, and the closing remarks

89) During an inspection, you see something that you don't understand. What should you do?

(A) If your client doesn't ask about it, just ignore it

(B) Make up something that sounds good

(C) Briefly note it but do not include on your report

(D) Tell your client that you don't know what it is but you will find out

90) Is the following statement a description, cause, implication, or a recommended action?

"These uneven stairs are a trip hazard"

(A) Description

(B) Cause

(C) Implication

(D) Recommended action

91) The Standards require:

(A) Conditions and causes

(B) Technically exhaustive inspections and descriptions

(C) Descriptions and causes

(D) Descriptions and conditions

92) What is EIFS is an example of:

(A) Interior wall surface material

(B) Exterior fasteners

(C) Exterior wall surface material

(D) Interior floor surface material

93) Building paper can be used instead of:

(A) Vapor barrier

(B) Moisture barrier

(C) Housewrap

(D) Shrinkwrap

94) Which of the following 3 components make up stucco?

(A) Water

(B) Super P

(C) Cement

(D) Aggregate

95) Which term is used to describe a flashing where wall extends beyond a roof, to shed water away from the stucco?

(A) Kickout

(B) Branchout

(C) Directional plate

(D) Corner flashing

96) While inspecting a home, you observe vines growing alongside the wood siding. What is the effect of this situation?

(A) Reduced curb appeal

(B) Reduction of offer price

(C) Increased mortar deterioration

(D) Reduced drying potential

97) What is a special characteristic about a siding nail?

(A) Sharpened head

(B) Rounded head

(C) Square head

(D) Countersunk head

98) The slope of a typical gutter slope should be:

(A) 1 inch drop over 50 inches run

(B) 1 inch drop over 100 inches run

(C) 1 inch drop over 150 inches run

(D) 1 inch drop over 200 inches run

99) While on an inspection, you observe a long row of new sod running in front of the house to the street. This could indicate:

(A) A new water or sewer line

(B) A new fertilization technique

(C) A new telephone line

(D) A new sump pump was installed

100) Garage floors should:

(A) Finished with a non-slip surface

(B) Be at least 5 inches think

(C) Sloped to drain

(D) Not have fire extinguishers

101) On an inspection, you observe a retaining wall that is leaning over but it is not cracked or damaged in any way. Which of the following is best to tell your client?

(A) The wall is in danger of falling over and include this in your report

(B) The wall should be investigated further by a specialist since it is impossible to tell from a single visit.

(C) The wall will fall over in the near future and to evacuate the home until then

(D) The wall should be investigated further by a specialist since you were able to tell from this single visit.

102) All of the following are common problem areas with respect to a roof, except:

(A) Changes in slope

(B) Flashings

(C) Changes in material

(D) Ridge vents

103) Wind is considered a dead load on a roof.

True or False?

104) What does the word "square" mean when discussing roofing material?

(A) 10 square feet

(B) 1 square foot

(C) 100 square feet

(D) 1000 square feet

105) During a roof inspection, you observe an area where there are dissimilar metal flashing, nail heads, metal hooks, and strips of metal. What might you suggest to your client?

(A) Inexperienced contractors

(B) The flashings should be replaced

(C) Patching might have been done

(D) An addition might have been built

106) Which one of the following is a buildup of ice at the bottom of a roof slope?

(A) Ice bridge

(B) Ice block

(C) Ice wall

(D) Ice dam

107) All of the following areas are prone to ice dams, except:

(A) North slopes

(B) Roofs with narrow soffits

(C) Low sloped roofs

(D) Roofs over balconies

108) It is possible to find three layers of asphalt shingles on a roof.

True or False?

109) What are 2 shapes of concrete tile?

(A) Curved or bull nosed

(B) Flat or hexagonal

(C) Flat or countersunk

(D) Flat or curved

110) Selvage roofing is known as:

(A) A cheap alternative

(B) Rolled roofing

(C) Crossed weaved valleys

(D) Recycled material

111) Which of the following is the result of moisture and is harmless?

(A) Black mold

(B) Termite infestation

(C) White mold

(D) Algae discoloration

112) Step flashings should be nailed to which of the following:

(A) The drywall

(B) The wall

(C) The roof

(D) The step threads

113) Which of the following is used to direct rain runoff into the gutters and away from the roof to protect the lower edge of the roof?

(A) Drip edge flashing

(B) Step flashing

(C) Kicker

(D) Toe nail flashing

114) If glass is angled more than a ———— degree slope, it should not be treated as a window.

(A) 5

(B) 10

(C) 15

(D) 20

115) All of the following are common footing types except:

(A) Piers

(B) Raised floor

(C) Piles

(D) Spread footings

116) Which of the followings is the thickening of a foundation wall to accommodate a concentrated load of a beam or column?

(A) Pile

(B) Pier

(C) Pilaster

(D) Footing

117) These types of cracks are typically caused by the natural curing of concrete.

(A) Shear cracks

(B) Stress cracks

(C) Settlement cracks

(D) Shrinkage cracks

118) During a home inspection, you observe what appear to be shrinkage cracks. What should you include in the report concerning its main implication?

(A) Leakage

(B) Minor structural problems

(C) Differential settlement

(D) Major structural problems

119) After a heavy rain, a client tells you that his damaged foundation wall has suddenly shifted. What could have caused this?

(A) Increased hydrostatic pressure and shrinkage of expansive soils

(B) Decreased hydrostatic pressure and swelling of expansive soils

(C) Increased Isobaric pressure and settlement of expansive soils

(D) Increased hydrostatic pressure and swelling of expansive soils

120) Which of the following is formed when a foundation is poured at two separate times and the first part has started to cure when the second part is being poured?

(A) Hot joint

(B) Amplitude

(C) Undercut

(D) Cold joint

121) What is the proper way to attach a sill to a foundation?

(A) Bolted

(B) Nailed

(C) Epoxy

(D) Floating

122) All of the following are acceptable ways to attach a steel column to a steel beam, except:

(A) Bolts

(B) Welds

(C) Bendable tabs

(D) Epoxy

123) At which located is a column most likely to rot?

(A) Bottom

(B) Top

(C) At connections

(D) Middle

124) A beam that is notched at the bottom is more likely to fail than one that is notched at the top.

True or False?

125) It is acceptable to shim a steel beam with wood.

True or False?

126) All of the following are functions of a joist, except:

(A) Transfer live loads to beams

(B) Transfer dead loads to foundations

(C) Transfer live loads to walls

(D) Transfer live loads directly to columns

127) What is the main purpose of insulation?

(A) To control heat gain

(B) To minimize convection

(C) To control heat loss

(D) To control latent heat of fusion

128) What are the three different modes of heat transfer?

(A) Conduction

(B) Evaporation

(C) Radiation

(D) Convection

129) What is the purpose of an air barrier?

(A) To stop air movement through the foundation

(B) To encourage air movement through building walls and roofs for ventilation

(C) To stop heat loss through building walls and roofs

(D) To stop air movement through building walls and roofs

130) When is it safe to omit a soffit vent?

(A) When gable venting is present at opposite ends

(B) When gable venting is present at the same end

(C) When an air barrier exists

(D) When the ventilation system is balanced

131) It is never possible to over-vent an attic.

True or False?

132) Which of the following items should you wear when inspecting an attic?

(A) Ventilator

(B) Goggles

(C) Long sleeves with tight cuffs

(D) Masks

133) Metal vents should have insulation that is installed this way:

(A) Insulation should not be installed near metal vents

(B) Contained in a boxed area to keep insulation in contact

(C) Contained in a boxed area to keep insulation away

(D) Contained together wrapped in an air barrier

134) Which is the following term describes when heat is transmitted by conduction directly from our feet to the floor?

(A) Cold transmission affect

(B) Cold feet affect

(C) Cold conduction affect

(D) Cold floor affect

Exam 2 Solutions:

Solution to Question # 68:

(D) Withdrawal.

Solution to Question # 69:

(B) Shear resistance.

Solution to Question # 70:

(B) It is dent resistant.

Aluminum siding can dent easily, and the damaged area may be difficult to repair or replace. Many siding manufacturers offer a thin backing board of insulation that fits behind each panel. This backing can help protect against dents.

Solution to Question # 71:

(C) The building sills and/or lower walls have been damaged by rot or pests.

Solution to Question # 72:

(D) To mix cold water in with outgoing hot water.

Anti-scald valves, also known as tempering valves and mixing valves, mix cold water in with outgoing hot water so that the hot water that leaves a fixture is not hot enough to scald a person.

Solution to Question # 73:

(A) Simple and inexpensive.

Solution to Question # 74:

(A) It can spread contaminated water back through a distribution system.

Backflow at uncontrolled cross connections can allow pollutants or contaminants to enter the potable water system. Sickness can result from ingesting water that has been contaminated due to backflow.

Solution to Question # 75:

(D) Backflow preventer.

Solution to Question # 76:

(B) The wiring should be evaluated by a qualified electrician.

If properly maintained, aluminum wiring is acceptable. You should note it and recommend to your client that they hire a qualified electrician inspect the wiring.

Solution to Question # 77:

(D) Carbon monoxide

Solution to Question # 78:

(C) 5 min.

Solution to Question # 79:

(B) Back-pressure.

This reduction in supply pressure occurs whenever the amount of water being used exceeds the amount of water being supplied (such as during water-line flushing, fire-fighting, or breaks in water mains).

Solution to Question # 80:

(C) A structural analysis of the framing.

If you observe an issue with the framing, always note it and recommend that a licensed professional engineer inspect it. (B) is true in the case where an attic is full of boxes an junk, you should note it is such on your report. You should never move items out of the way.

Solution to Question # 81:

(D) Back-siphonage.

Back-siphonage can occur when there is a high velocity in a pipe line, when there is a line repair or break that is lower than a service point, or when there is lowered main pressure due to high-water withdrawal rate (such as during fire-fighting or water-main flushing).

Solution to Question # 82:

False.

Solution to Question # 83:

(A) 2 ½ hours.

Any more time could be considered technically exhaustive. You should explain this upfront to manage expectations.

Solution to Question # 84:

(B) A home inspector is not required to report causes of conditions.

You do not need to report on what you think the cause of a deficiency is, you do have to observe it, note the implications of the deficiency.

Solution to Question # 85:

(D) Your friend who is a general contractor.

It is unethical to be referring work to your friends to your client.

Solution to Question # 86:

False.

That is the definition of an Appraisal.

Solution to Question # 87:

(B) To reduce liability.

If you can explain the expectations to your client before the inspection and also explain your observations during the inspection, you will decrease your chances of a claim in the future. Involve your client throughout the process and try to teach him something new. Give him information and he will feel like he got value of his investment. Opportunity to adjust his expectations.

Solution to Question # 88:

(D) 4: Pre inspection routine, opening remarks, inspection itself, and the closing remarks

The pre inspection routine is just as important as any the other 3 parts. This is where you can adjust your clients expectations, arrive early, et read, time is valuable. You need to sell the inspection.

Solution to Question # 89:

(D) Tell your client that you don't know what it is but you will find out.

Always be ethical and never try to hide something. You will gain your client's respect for doing extra homework and providing an answer the next day.

Solution to Question # 90:

(C) Implication

Solution to Question # 91:

(D) Descriptions and conditions.

Solution to Question # 92:

(C) Exterior wall surface material.

Solution to Question # 93:

(C) Housewrap.

Solution to Question # 94:

(A), (C), and (D).

Solution to Question # 95:

(A) Kickout.

Solution to Question # 96:

(D) Reduced drying potential.

The drying potential is reduced because vines hold water. Recommend that they be cut back away from the house and that there may be concealed water intrusion into the home that you cannot see.

Solution to Question # 97:

(B) Rounded head.

The rounded head holds the board on top away from the board underneath, which promotes drying potential.

Solution to Question # 98:

(D) 1 inch drop over 200 inches run.

Solution to Question # 99:

(A) A new water or sewer line.

Solution to Question # 100:

(C) To drain.

Usually towards the door.

Solution to Question # 101:

(B) The wall should be investigated further by a specialist since it is impossible to tell from a single visit.

Solution to Question # 102:

(D) Ridge vents.

The highest percentages of problem areas are changes in slope and material, and flashings (either installed incorrectly or deteriorating).

Solution to Question # 103:

False.

Dead loads are permanent loads imposed on the structure by the building materials. Wind is an example of a live load.

Solution to Question # 104:

(C) 100 square feet.

The amount of building material required to cover 100 square feet of roof surface with the proper material exposure.

Solution to Question # 105:

(C) Patching might have been done.

Other signs might have been Caulking, differences in color, texture, size, or style. Also, if there are different roofing materials.

Solution to Question # 106:

(D) Ice dam.

They are caused by heat escaping from the house and melting the snow on the upper parts of the house.

Solution to Question # 107:

(B) Roofs with narrow soffits.

Other areas include: Bottom of valleys, roofs with change slope near the eaves, roofs with wide soffits, roofs over porches.

Solution to Question # 108:

True.

Solution to Question # 109:

(D) Flat or curved.

Solution to Question # 110:

(B) Rolled roofing.

Solution to Question # 111:

(D) Algae discoloration.

Solution to Question # 112:

A and B are correct. It could be nailed to either the wall or the roof, but usually the roof.

Solution to Question # 113:

(A) Drip edge flashing.

Solution to Question # 114:

(C) 15.

Windows should not be used as skylights.

Solution to Question # 115:

(B) Raised floor.

Solution to Question # 116:

(C) Pilaster

Solution to Question # 117:

(D) Shrinkage cracks.

Shrinkage cracks usually show up within the first year of the life of a home. They mostly occur at stress concentration points, such at the corners of window openings.

Solution to Question # 118:

(A) Leakage.

Solution to Question # 119:

(D) Increased hydrostatic pressure and swelling of expansive soils.

Solution to Question # 120:

(C) Cold joint.

A cold joint is located in the intersection of the first and second parts.

Solution to Question # 121:

(A) Bolted.

Sill are to be anchored to the foundation using anchor bolts.

Solution to Question # 122:

(D) Epoxy.

Solution to Question # 123:

(A) Bottom.

Solution to Question # 124:

True.

Solution to Question # 125:

False.

Solution to Question # 126:

(D) Transfer live loads directly to columns.

Solution to Question # 127:

(C) To control heat loss.

<u>Solution to Question # 128:</u>

A, C, and D are correct.

Evaporation only applied to people.

<u>Solution to Question # 129:</u>

(D) To stop air movement through building walls and roofs.

<u>Solution to Question # 130:</u>

(A) When gable venting is present at opposite ends.

<u>Solution to Question # 131:</u>

False.

Over-venting is possible if the ceiling is not sealed very well which can cause negative pressure in the attic space and introduce warm moist air at a faster rate.

<u>Solution to Question # 132:</u>

B, C, and D are correct.

<u>Solution to Question # 133:</u>

(C) Contained in a boxed area to keep insulation away.

<u>Solution to Question # 134:</u>

(D) Cold floor affect.

135) All of the following are signs of high humidity in a home, except:

(A) Stale odors

(B) Stuffy air

(C) Electrical corrosion

(D) Condensation on windows

136) What are the two main items you should be looking for on ducts in attics?

(A) Insulation and air/vapor barrier

(B) Vapor retarder and hangers

(C) Insulation and solar reflective barrier

(D) GCFI outlets and air/vapor barrier

137) A balanced ventilation systems refers to:

(A) Maximizing the exhaust air while minimizing the fresh air supply

(B) Controlling both the exhaust and fresh air supply

(C) Maximizing the fresh air while minimizing the exhaust air supply

(D) Controlling the heat loss

138) What does the term "drying potential" mean?

(A) The ability of a material to maintain its moisture after it has gotten wet

(B) The ability of a material to avoid becoming wet

(C) The ability of a material to dry out during curing phase

(D) The ability of a material to dry out after it has gotten wet

139) Which of the following types of walls are located between attached dwellings units, and act as a sound and fire separation.

(A) Divider wall

(B) Knee wall

(C) Separator wall

(D) Party wall

140) What are two problems that are common to party walls?

(A) Ice dams and mold

(B) Not continuous and ice dams

(C) Ice dams and ventilation

(D) Not continuous and sagging

141) Which of the following terms associated with stairs is the width of the place that where you put your foot on?

(A) Run

(B) Winder depth

(C) Stringer

(D) Tread depth

142) What home problem is the most common complaint against home inspectors?

(A) Humidity levels

(B) Wet basements

(C) Foundation cracks

(D) Water heater issues

143) Dehumidifiers are not an effective way to fix wet basement problems.

True or False?

144) If a window if too low on a stairwell or landing, what is the possible danger?

(A) Someone will not be able to see out of the window

(B) Someone could trip on the stairs and fall out of the window

(C) Someone could climb up from the outside into the window

(D) Someone could trip on the stairs and damage the opening mechanism on the window

145) On a wood frame flooring system, where is rot most likely to occur?

(A) Around plumbing fixtures

(B) Around ventilation vents

(C) Around electrical devices

(D) Around tile joints.

146) Which of the following is a metal ceiling problem?

(A) Rust

(B) Corrosion

(C) Loose clips

(D) Sagging

147) Which of the following terms describes creating a location where you want a concrete slab to crack.

(A) Stress joint

(B) Control joint

(C) Concrete joint

(D) Expansion joint

148) All of the following are plaster and drywall ceiling problems, except:

(A) Sag

(B) Nail pops

(C) Mold growth

(D) Shadow effect

149) Service entrance conductors run from the service drop to this:

(A) The receptacles

(B) The electric company

(C) The service panel

(D) The service meter

150) How is the service size the service determined?

(A) By voltage and amperage ratings

(B) By amperage rating only

(C) By voltage rating only

(D) By amperage ratings and payment schedule

151) Electrical wiring in a house is alternating current.

True or False?

152) What is the voltage for a typical large appliance?

(A) 120 volts

(B) 425 volts

(C) 220 volts

(D) 240 volts

153) As a home inspector, it is required for you to perform a load calculation if the client requests it.

True or False?

154) 120-volt service can be determined by how many wires?

(A) 4 wires

(B) 2 wires

(C) 3 wires

(D) Cannot be determined by the number of wires

155) Which of the following terms prevent water entry into the service entrance conductors?

(A) Drip loop

(B) Entrance loop

(C)Weather loop

(D) U-loop

156) Less than an amp of electrical current can kill someone?

True or False?

157) In terms of fuses, which of the following is a safety concern?

(A) A fuse that missing

(B) A fuse that is too big

(C) A fuse that is replaced with a circuit breaker

(D) A fuse that is too small

158) Which of the following terms means connecting things to zero electrical potential?

(A) Bonding

(B) Neutralizing

(C) Shorting

(D) Grounding

159) Which of the following terms means connecting things to similar electrical potential?

(A) Grounding

(B) Bonding

(C) Shorting

(D) Neutralizing

160) Which is the proper way to handle an abandoned wire?

(A) Tag it

(B) Remove it

(C) Color it

(D) Ground it

161) On gas piping, this is installed in order to collect dirt and separating it from the gas before the gas valve.

(A) Dead leg

(B) Drip hand

(C) Drip valve

(D) Drip leg

162) Carbon monoxide is the result of natural gas which has undergone:

(A) Insufficient combustion

(B) Incomplete combustion

(C) Back drafting

(D) Spillage

163) Ribbon burners tend to be larger output than mono-part burners.

True or False?

164) In a gas furnace, if the heat exchanger has failed, what will be the most likely result if the blower turns on?

(A) Carbon monoxide poisoning

(B) Spillage

(C) Waving flame over one burner

(D) Fire

165) Most conventional gas furnaces have this number of panel covers.

(A) One

(B) Three

(C) Five

(D) Two

166) How might you visually inspect for a heat exchanger failure when the house air fan turns on?

(A) Observe the flame pattern of the gas furnace

(B) Observe the time stamp for the life of the gas furnace

(C) Observe the electrical output of the gas furnace

(D) Observe the temperature difference of the gas furnace

167) What is term used to describe when combustion products flow out of the furnace into the room through the burner or draft hood, rather up through the vent?

(A) Combustion venting

(B) Back drafting

(C) Up drafting

(D) Unlawful venting

168) All of the following are common problems with furnace blowers, except:

(A) Poorly secured

(B) Unbalanced

(C) Worn belt

(D) Installed backwards

169) Why might you look up into the chimney clean out if it is below the vent connection to the chimney? Choose two that apply.

(A) To check the connection between the vent connector and the chimney

(B) To measure the inner diameter of the flume against code

(C) To check to backdraft

(D) To check for obstructions

170) It is a requirement to estimate the life expectancy of a furnace on your inspections.

True or False?

171) A conventional gas furnace has a typical life span of how many years?

(A) 20 to 25

(B) 26 to 30

(C) 31 to 35

(D) 15 to 19

172) What will most likely happen if a furnace vent dischargers condensate just below a building soffit?

(A) Cause the grade to erode overtime

(B) Cause backdrafting since it is installed incorrectly

(C) Cause the soffit to rot overtime

(D) Cause the vent to rust overtime

173) For an exterior, above ground oil storage tank, the supply line size is typically 3/8 inches.

True or False?

174) Which of the following is not a concern for an abandoned buried oil tank?

(A) Environmental issues

(B) Settlement

(C) Removing the tank

(D) Clean-up costs

175) Conventional furnaces are forced draft for what type of burners?

(A) Natural gas burners

(B) Convection burners

(C) Oil burners

(D) Heat exchanger burners

176) What is the usual pump pressure for a residential oil burner pump?

(A) 12 psi

(B) 50 psi

(C) 120 psi

(D) 80 psi

177) What protects the steel of the furnace from the high temperature flame in an oil furnace?

(A) A reflationary

(B) A refractory

(C) A relamination tile

(D) A reveling agent

178) What ensures adequate draft air supply for a chimney?

(A) Chimney damper

(B) Air damper

(C) Pressure damper

(D) Barometric damper

179) Which material will you least likely find used as an exhaust vent material?

(A) Aluminum

(B) Steel

(C) Plastic

(D) ABS

180) Power vents are sometimes allowed on conventional oil furnace vent connectors.

True or False?

181) Copper tube boilers have what characteristic as compared to cast-iron boilers?

(A) Longer life span

(B) Less expensive

(C) Better heat transfer

(D) More salvage value

182) A boiler has a typically operating pressure of usually:

(A) 12 to 15 psi

(B) 7 to 11 psi

(C) 17 to 21 psi

(D) 4 to 7 psi

1

83) All of the following are safety controls found on all hydronic systems, except:

(A) Backflow preventer

(B) High temperature limit

(C) Pressure relief valve

(D) Backdaft preventer

184) It is a requirement to test a pressure-relief valve.

True or False?

185) On a hot water boiler, where is the pressure relief valve located?

(A) On bottom of the boiler

(B) On the side of the boiler

(C) There is no pressure relief valve for a water boiler

(D) On top of the boiler

186) The high temperature limit switch is usually set to which of the following control settings for a water boiler?

(A) 110 °

(B) 210 °

(C) 310 °

(D) 75 °

187) Where is the best location to place a radiator in a room?

(A) On an exterior wall

(B) On an interior wall below a window

(C) On the floor of the middle of the room

(D) On an exterior wall below a window

188) For a tankless coil heater, which of the following valves are used to reduce the temperature of the domestic water below the boiler water temperature to prevent scalding?

(A) Mixing valve

(B) Combination valve

(C) Pressure relief valve

(D) Isothermal valve

189) What is the typical lifespan of a cast iron boiler?

(A) 15 to 30 years

(B) 10 to 25 years

(C) 35 to 50 years

(D) 40 to 50 years

190) Since there are no radiators, radiant piping systems do not need bleed valves.

True or False?

191) What is an interior passage within a chimney which moves gases upwards from different fuel burning devices?

(A) A vent

(B) A flue

(C) An illegal installation

(D) A Chimney

192) Which of the following may damage the masonry in a chimney?

(A) Carbon Monoxide

(B) Condensation

(C) Vapor gas

(D) Rodents

193) Fuels, such as, natural gas and propane, typically require what kind of vent?

(A) L vents

(B) S vents

(C) B vents

(D) A vents

194) Fuels, such as, gas and oil, typically require what kind of vent?

(A) Z vents

(B) S vents

(C) B vents

(D) L vents

195) If a chimney is classified as "type A", it can be determined that it is used for this type of fuel?

(A) Oil and wood burning appliances

(B) Propane and wood burning appliances

(C) Gas and wood burning appliances

(D) Wood burning appliances only

196) Which of the following limits is true regarding laterally supporting a metal chimney?

(A) > 10 feet

(B) > 5 feet

(C) > 2.5 feet

(D) > 15 feet

197) A metal chimney will most likely rust at this location?

(A) At the vent joint

(B) Below the roof line

(C) At the top of the stack

(D) Above the roof line

198) It is common practice to weld sections of a chimney together on site.

True or False?

199) Which of the following switches is used to protect the elements from overheating by making sure there is adequate airflow across them?

(A) Override switch

(B) Surf switch

(C) Relief switch

(D) Sail switch

200) On a fireplace, what is the term used to collect ashes so that they can easily be removed?

(A) Garbage pit

(B) Alternating pit

(C) Ashpit

(D) Sump pit

Exam # 3 Solutions:

Solution to Question # 135:

(C) Electrical corrosion.

Solution to Question # 136:

(A) Insulation and air/vapor barrier.

Solution to Question # 137:

(B) Controlling both the exhaust and fresh air supply.

Solution to Question # 138:

(D) The ability of a material to dry out after it has gotten wet.

Solution to Question # 139:

(D) Party wall.

Common materials are masonry block and wood frame with drywall.

Solution to Question # 140:

(B) Not continuous and ice dams.

Solution to Question # 141:

(D) Tread depth.

Winder is a tread that tapers to a point. Stringer is the support for the treads. Run is the horizontal offset between steps.

Solution to Question # 142:

(B) Wet basements.

Solution to Question # 143:

True.

Solution to Question # 144:

(B) Someone could trip on the stairs and fall out of the window.

Solution to Question # 145:

(A) Around plumbing fixtures.

Especially around toilets.

Solution to Question # 146:

(A) Rust.

Solution to Question # 147:

(C) Control joint.

The purpose of the control joint is purposely creating a stress concentration joint. If the concrete is going to crack, you want it to crack here.

Solution to Question # 148:

(A), (B), and (D) are correct.

(C) Mold growth is an implication of common wall problems.

Solution to Question # 149:

(C) The service panel.

Solution to Question # 150:

(A) By voltage and amperage ratings.

Solution to Question # 151:

True.

Direct current usually comes from a battery source.

Solution to Question # 152

(D) 240 volts.

Solution to Question # 153:

False.

Solution to Question # 154

(B) 2 wires.

Solution to Question # 155:

(A) Drop loop.

The drip look also shows that the wires are not pulling tight and being strained at the splices.

Solution to Question # 156

True.

Solution to Question # 157:

(B) A fuse that is too big.

Thus allowing more current to enter the circuit. It is better to undersize a fuse than oversize.

Solution to Question # 158:

(D) Grounding.

Solution to Question # 159:

(B) Bonding.

Solution to Question # 160:

(B) Remove it.

All abandoned wires should be totally removed out of service.

Solution to Question # 161:

(D) Drip leg.

Solution to Question # 162:

(B) Incomplete combustion.

Solution to Question # 163:

False.

Solution to Question # 164:

(C) Waving flame over one burner.

Solution to Question # 165:

(D) Two.

Compartment doors for the blower and burner.

Solution to Question # 166:

(A) Observe the flame pattern of the gas furnace.

Solution to Question # 167:

(B) Backdrafting.

Also known as "spillage". This is a life-threatening situation.

Solution to Question # 168:

(D) Installed backwards.

Installed backwards is a common problem observed for mechanical filters.

Solution to Question # 169:

(A) and (D) are correct.

Solution to Question # 170:

False.

It is advised, however, to report if the system is near the end of its useful life.

Solution to Question # 171:

(A) 20 to 25.

Solution to Question # 172:

(C) Cause the soffit to rot overtime.

Solution to Question # 173:

False.

The line size if usually 2 inches in order to allow the oil to flow at lower temperatures, since oil becomes viscous at low temperatures.

Solution to Question # 174:

(B) Settlement.

Solution to Question # 175:

(C) Oil burners.

Solution to Question # 176:

(D) 80 psi.

Solution to Question # 177:

(B) A refractory.

Solution to Question # 178:

(D) Barometric damper.

Solution to Question # 179:

(A) Aluminum.

This is because oil combustion gases are hotter than natural gas combustion gases.

Solution to Question # 180:

True.

Solution to Question # 181:

(C) Better heat transfer.

Solution to Question # 182:

(A) 12 to 15 psi.

Solution to Question # 183:

(D) Backdaft preventer.

Also, low water cutout is a safety control.

Solution to Question # 184:

False.

Solution to Question # 185:

(D) On top of the boiler.

It will also typically discharge near the floor area.

Solution to Question # 186:

(B) 210 °.

Solution to Question # 187:

(D) On an exterior wall below a window.

This location is used because it creates greater comfort, by counteracting the cold down draught, which is especially prevalent with single-glazed windows. The second reason for locating radiators under windows is that it allows greater flexibility when arranging furniture, which one does not normally place beneath windows.

Solution to Question # 188:

(A) Mixing valve.

Solution to Question # 189:

(C) 35 to 50 years.

Solution to Question # 190:

False.

Solution to Question # 191:

(B) A flue.

Solution to Question # 192:

(B) Condensation.

Solution to Question # 193:

(C) B vents.

Solution to Question # 194:

(D) L vents.

Solution to Question # 195:

(A) Oil and wood burning appliances.

Solution to Question # 196:

(B) > 5 feet.

Solution to Question # 197:

(D) Above the roof line.

Solution to Question # 198:

False.

Solution to Question # 199:

(D) Sail switch.

Solution to Question # 200:

(C) Ashpit.

201) The purpose of a firebox is to:

(A) Spread the fire

(B) Contain the fire

(C) Prevent backdraft

(D) Introduce supply air

202) What is the maximum angle that a chimney is allowed to be offset from the vertical?

(A) 10°

(B) 20°

(C) 30°

(D) 40°

203) Freon is in which state when it is in the suction line?

(A) Vapor

(B) Gas

(C) Liquid

(D) Transient

204) When Freon leaves the compressor, what is its temperature range?

(A) 20- 40 °F

(B) 170- 230 °F

(C) 100 °F

(D) 50 °F

205) As gas gets compressed, it cools down.

True or False?

206) An oversized air conditioner is better than an undersized one.

True or False?

207) When the system is operating, which one of the refrigerant lines will feel warm?

(A) Suction Line

(B) Evaporator Line

(C) Liquid line

(D) Solid line

208) Which refrigerant line should be insulated?

(A) Suction line

(B) Liquid line

(C) Electrical line

(D) No line should be insulated

209) Refrigerant lines are usually made of this type of material ?

(A) Copper

(B) Aluminum

(C) Steel

(D) Plastic

210) If there is no return air grille in a bedroom, the door should be which of the following?

(A) Removed

(B) Sanded

(C) Undercut

(D) Overcut

211) How are heat pumps generally sized?

(A) Based on the cooling load

(B) Based on the heating load

(C) Based on the air conditioner load

(D) Based on the appliance load

212) Which of the following keeps the oil at the base of the compressor warm enough to boil off the refrigerant?

(A) Dip stick heater

(B) Oil heater

(C) Engine heater

(D) Crankcase heater

213) According to the scope of a standard home inspection, you are required to evaluate the quality of the water available at a private source.

True or False?

214) Water service piping used in modern construction is typically what size?

(A) ¼"

(B) ¾"

(C) ½"

(D) 2/3"

215) Which type of valve shuts off the water supply and allows the system plumbing to be drained?

(A) Stop and waste valve

(B) Block and waste valve

(C) Stop and plug valve

(D) Trap and waste valve

216) Copper piping requires a vertical support at what interval?

(A) At least every 3 feet

(B) At least every 5 feet

(C) At least every 8 feet

(D) At least every 10 feet

217) Plastic piping needs more support than copper piping because it tends to expand more.

True or False?

218) Which type of connection is a piping arrangement in which waste can back up into the supply piping and contaminate it when the pressure drops on the supply side.

(A) Hot connection

(B) Mixed connection

(C) Straight connection

(D) Cross connection

219) Why is it not usually not acceptable to use plastic pipe between units in shared dwellings?

(A) Because it is expensive

(B) Because it is combustible

(C) Because it has to be insulated

(D) Because it is not accessible to be repaired

220) Vertical pipes at ends of runs are one method of preventing which of the following?

(A) Water pressure built up

(B) Leakage

(C) Water hammer

(D) Temperature rise

221) Which two of the following methods are used to determine the rating of a water heater?

(A) The static pressure in the tank

(B) The volume of water it can hold

(C) The temperature gradient

(D) The size of the burner

222) When two water heaters are installed side by side, the piping should be installed in this way:

(A) In parallel

(B) Cross flow

(C) In series

(D) Double walled piping

223) Which one of the following reasons explains why a toilet does not need a trap?

(A) Because codes inspectors cannot see it for conformance

(B) The trap would not seal against sewer gases

(C) A trap would create back pressure and could not flush

(D) The bowl itself is a trap

224) The typical vent size on a sewage ejector pump is:

(A) 1 inch

(B) 2 inches

(C) 1/4 inch

(D) 1/2 inch

225) What are the two main types of roofing systems?

(A) Sloped roofs

(B) Cathedral roofs

(C) Flat roofs

(D) Inverted roofs

226) The slope of a roof is typically called the:

(A) Run

(B) Angle

(C) Rise

(D) Pitch

227) Which of the following slopes is considered a low slope?

(A) 4 in 12 and up

(B) 2 in 12 to 4 in 12

(C) 2 in 10 to 4 in 10

(D) 0 in 12 to 2 in 12

228) How do you calculate the slope of a roof?

(A) Run/rise

(B) Rise/pitch

(C) Rise/run

(D) Run/angle

229) Roofs with a pitch greater than four in twelve are considered this kind of roof system:

(A) Flat

(B) Low

(C) High

(D) Conventional

230) The steeper the pitch of the roof, the longer the shingles will last.

True or False?

231) The granular material on asphalt shingles protect it from:

(A) Rain

(B) Ultra violet light

(C) Humidity

(D) Convection radiation

232) Which of the following is one of the biggest enemies of asphalt roofs?

(A) Foot traffic

(B) Snow

(C) Rain

(D) Sunlight

233) What is the life expectancy of wood shingles?

(A) 10 to 20 years

(B) 20 to 30 years

(C) 30 to 40 years

(D) 40 to 50 years

234) High quality slate roofs have an average life expectancy of:

(A) 30 to 70 years

(B) 40 to 80 years

(C) 50 to 90 years

(D) 60 to 100 years

235) Why are concrete and clay tiles notoriously difficult to flash?

(A) They are not flat

(B) They are heavy

(C) They are not self-sealing

(D) They are porous

236) Which of the following roof coverings often discolor and promote the growth of fungus or moss?

(A) Clay tiles

(B) Slate shingles

(C) Asbestos cement shingles

(D) Wood shingles

237) Metal roofs should be covered with tar in order to seal the surface.

True or False?

238) Built up roofs are commonly called:

(A) Vertical roofs

(B) Self sealing

(C) Tar and gravel roofs

(D) Gravel and rock roofs

239) A lack of gravel in built-up roofing can cause rapid deterioration of the roof surface. Which of the following is a condition that occurs as the surface breaks down and dehydrates due to exposure to sunlight.

(A) Dogging

(B) Birding

(C) Crocodiling

(D) Alligatoring

240) Roll roofing is sometimes known as:

(A) Reroofing

(B) Short rolls

(C) Steep roof installations

(D) Selvage roofing

241) A water stain on a ceiling of a built-up roof indicates a leak immediately above.

True or False?

242) Which of the following is an alternative to built-up roofing?

(A) Unmodified Bitumen

(B) Bitumen Gravel

(C) Insulated Bitumen

(D) Modified Bitumen

243) As a general rule, shedding type roofs should have a slope of:

(A) Four in twelve or more

(B) Two in twelve or more

(C) Six in twelve or more

(D) Four in twelve or less

244) An asphalt shingle roof can be installed immediately over one other layer of asphalt shingles.

True or False?

245) Choose two typically vulnerable areas of a roof:

(A) Changes in roof direction

(B) Changes in material color

(C) At the drip edge

(D) Changes in materials occurs

246) Effective solutions to ice damming problems are increased:

(A) Attic insulation and insulation

(B) Ventilation and humidity

(C) Attic insulation and ventilation

(D) Ventilation and waterproof membrane

247) How wide are metal valley flashings?

(A) 2 inches wide

(B) 8 inches wide

(C) 12 inches wide

(D) 24 inches wide

248) In most cases, the condition of hip and ridge flashings is not a major concern since water is always shed away from them.

True or False?

249) What is the portion of a chimney flashing that is most prone to leakage?

(A) The portion facing the low section of roofing

(B) The portion mid-section of roofing

(C) The portion facing the high section of roofing

(D) The portion below the chimney

250) If wood siding is used as a material on a dormer, how high above the main roof surface should it stop so that rot does not occur?

(A) ¼" inch

(B) 1 inch

(C) 2 inches

(D) ½" inch

251) Where a roof meets a parapet wall, what is required?

(A) Emergency ladder

(B) Flashings

(C) Vent

(D) Grounding electrode

252) It is not uncommon for this to form on the interior of skylights:

(A) Mold

(B) Condensation

(C) Carbon Monoxide

(D) Cracks

253) This metal flashing is provided along the lower edge of some sloped roofs and is intended to direct water from the roof edge into the gutters without damaging the fascia or roof sheathing edges.

(A) Bottom edge

(B) Kick edge

(C) Skylight edge

(D) Drip edge

254) Chimneys of insufficient height are prone to:

(A) Leakage problems

(B) Updraft problems

(C) Downdraft problems

(D) Structural problems

255) Chimneys should be a minimum of three feet above the point of penetration through the roof and two feet higher than anything within:

(A) 5 feet of them

(B) 10 feet of them

(C) 15 feet of them

(D) 20 feet of them

256) Steep, simple roofs are more likely to develop problems than roofs with a variety of slopes, angles, and penetrations.

True or False?

257) If all the parts are doing their job, the exterior components of a building work together to provide:

(A) Aesthetically pleasing look

(B) Weathertight skin

(C) Insulated skin

(D) Watertight membrane

258) Typically, what are the most neglected parts of a home?

(A) Air conditioners

(B) Water heaters

(C) Exterior components

(D) Foundation cracks

259) What are the two most common sizes of gutters?

(A) 2-inch width

(B) 3-inch width

(C) 4-inch width

(D) 5-inch width

260) What is the most common problem with gutters?

(A) Leakage

(B) Structural damage

(C) Sagging

(D) Wet basements

261) As a general rule, a downspout should be provided for every:

(A) 10 feet of gutters

(B) 25 feet of gutters

(C) 40 feet of gutters

(D) 30 feet of gutters

262) Aluminum gutters often rust.

True or False?

263) It can be determined by a visual inspection that a underground drain is plugged or broken.

True or False?

264) Why is it best to extend the downspout along the lower roof to discharge directly into the lower roof gutter?

(A) The section of the lower roof cannot handle the additional dead load of the water

(B) The section of the lower roof in the path of the water will deteriorate quickly

(C) The section of the lower roof in the path of the water will cause leakage

(D) It is cheaper to do it this way

265) Some foundation wall systems are completely impervious to water.

True or False?

266) Why is the presence of mature trees and heavy vegetation on a steeply sloped portion of a lot a good sign?

(A) They add to curb appeal

(B) They mean the ground water is low

(C) They produce shade

(D) They reduce erosion

267) What material are window wells most often constructed of?

(A) Concrete and corrugated steel shell

(B) Plastic and corrugated steel shell

(C) Concrete and corrugated plastic shell

(D) Aluminum and corrugated steel shell

Solutions to Exam # 4:

Solution to Question # 201:

(B) Contain the fire.

Solution to Question # 202:

(C) 30°.

Solution to Question # 203:

(B) Gas.

Low temperature and pressure.

Solution to Question # 204:

(B) 170- 230 °F.

(A) 20- 40 °F is the temperature as it enters the evaporator coil. (C) 100 °F is the temperature as it leaves condenser coil. (D) 50 °F is the temperature as it enters the compressor.

Solution to Question # 205:

False.

Solution to Question # 206:

False.

Solution to Question # 207:

(C) Liquid line.

The suction line will feel cool.

Solution to Question # 208:

(A) Suction line.

Solution to Question # 209:

(A) Copper.

Solution to Question # 210:

(C) Undercut.

The room will overheat because the room becomes pressurized, which prevents cool air from entering.

Solution to Question # 211:

(A) Based on the cooling load.

Solution to Question # 212:

(D) Crankcase heater.

Also called a sump.

Solution to Question # 213:

False.

Solution to Question # 214:

(B) ¾".

Solution to Question # 215:

(A) Stop and waste valve.

Solution to Question # 216:

(D) At least every 10 feet.

Or every floor level.

Solution to Question # 217:

True.

Solution to Question # 218:

(D) Cross connection.

Solution to Question # 219:

(B) Because it is combustible.

Solution to Question # 220:

(C) Water hammer.

Solution to Question # 221:

(B) and (D) are correct.

Solution to Question # 222:

(A) In parallel.

Piping should be arranged so that the heaters are installed in parallel rather than in series, with equal length piping.

Solution to Question # 223:

(D) The bowl itself is a trap.

Solution to Question # 224:

(B) 2 inches.

Solution to Question # 225:

(A) and (C) are correct.

Sloped roofs are not water tight, but are designed to shed water like a pyramid of umbrellas. Flat roofs are watertight membranes.

Solution to Question # 226:

(D) Pitch.

Solution to Question # 227:

(B) 2 in 12 to 4 in 12.

Solution to Question # 228:

(C) Rise/run.

Solution to Question # 229:

(D) Conventional.

Solution to Question # 230:

True.

Solution to Question # 231:

(B) Ultra violet light.

Solution to Question # 232:

(D) Sunlight.

Solution to Question # 233:

(C) 30 to 40 years.

Solution to Question # 234:

(D) 60 to 100 years.

Solution to Question # 235:

(A) They are not flat.

Solution to Question # 236:

(C) Asbestos cement shingles.

They are not very common and are brittle and susceptible to mechanical damage.

Solution to Question # 237:

False.

Metal roofs should never be covered with tar as moisture trapped below the tar causes accelerated rusting.

Solution to Question # 238:

(C) Tar and gravel roofs.

Solution to Question # 239:

(D) Alligatoring.

Solution to Question # 240:

(D) Selvage roofing.

Solution to Question # 241:

False.

Because of the construction of a built-up roof, water can travel a significant distance though the plys of a roof before emerging on the interior.

Solution to Question # 242:

(D) Modified Bitumen.

Solution to Question # 243:

(A) Four in twelve or more.

Solution to Question # 244:

True. Although it is better to remove the old roofing first.

Solution to Question # 245:

(A) and (D) are correct.

For example, where a roof meets a chimney or a wall and where two or more flashings intersect (a chimney occurs in a valley)

Solution to Question # 246:

(C) Attic insulation and ventilation.

Solution to Question # 247:

(D) 24 inches wide.

However, the majority of the material cannot be seen, as it is hidden under the shingles.

Solution to Question # 248:

True.

Solution to Question # 249:

(C) The portion facing the high section of roofing.

Water running off a roof hits the high side and must be diverted around the chimney. Therefore, flashings on the high side should be a minimum of six inches in height or one-sixth of the width of the chimney, whichever is greater.

Solution to Question # 250:

(C) 2 inches.

Solution to Question # 251:

(B) Flashings.

Parapet wall flashings are often loose, deteriorated or missing altogether.

Solution to Question # 252:

(B) Condensation. Condensation is often mistaken for flashing leakage problems.

Solution to Question # 253:

(D) Drip edge.

If it is not installed properly, it can cause water damage to the eaves.

Solution to Question # 254:

(C) Downdraft problems.

Solution to Question # 255:

(B) 10 feet of them.

Solution to Question # 256:

False.

Solution to Question # 257:

(B) Weathertight skin.

Solution to Question # 258:

(C) Exterior components.

Solution to Question # 259:

(C) and (D) are correct.

Solution to Question # 260:

(A) Leakage.

Leakage will occur with galvanized gutters as they rust through. All types of gutters are prone to leakage at the joints. The most important function of a gutter is to ensure a dry basement.

Solution to Question # 261:

(C) 40 feet of gutters. On many houses, the number of downspouts is inadequate.

Solution to Question # 262:

False.

Aluminum gutters do not rust but they dent easily. They are also pre-finished and require low maintenance. Life expectancy is estimated to be 20 to 25 years.

Solution to Question # 263:

False.

If an underground drain malfunctions, water problems will likely develop in the basement in the area of the downspout.

Solution to Question # 264:

(B) The section of the lower roof in the path of the water will deteriorate quickly.

Solution to Question # 265:

False.

The likelihood of water penetration problems into basements and crawl spaces is partially dependent upon the grading of the lot adjacent to the foundation.

Solution to Question # 266:

(D) They reduce erosion.

Remember, it is not possible to determine the rate of erosion from a one-time visit.

Solution to Question # 267:

(A) Concrete and corrugated steel shell.

268) Since most bricks are not designed to be in contact with the soil, how many inches should they be kept above grade?

(A) 2 inches

(B) 4 inches

(C) 6 inches

(D) 8 inches

269) Mortar deterioration is more common than brick deterioration.

True or False?

270) In terms are stucco, why do cracks and bulges often appear near the floor level?

(A) Nails can expand in this area

(B) Wood framing members shrink in this area

(C) Water penetration is likely in this area

(D) The finisher usually neglect workmanship this area

271) What is the shape of siding nails that allows air circulation?

(A) Convex heads

(B) Square heads

(C) Counter sunk heads

(D) Rounded heads

272) How high should wood siding be above the soil?

(A) At least 5 inches

(B) At least 8 inches

(C) At least 4 inches

(D) At least 6 inches

273) Metal siding, particular aluminum, is prone to which of the following?

(A) Denting

(B) Rust

(C) Buckling

(D) Shearing

274) The most common problems associates with wood steps are:

(A) Slope and attack by insects

(B) Rot and misalignment

(C) Attack by insects and undersized

(D) Rot and attack by insects

275) How many feet, roughly, should footings be below the frost line?

(A) 2 feet

(B) 4 feet

(C) 6 feet

(D) 8 feet

276) which of the following are two basic forces?

(A) Compression and shear

(B) Compression and tension

(C) Tension and bending

(D) Tension and torsion

277) A material is under this type of force when it is being pulled apart from both ends:

(A) Compression

(B) Shear

(C) Torsion

(D) Tension

278) A material is under this type of force when it is being pushed together from both ends:

(A) Compression

(B) Shear

(C) Torsion

(D) Tension

279) Which of the following types of materials do not bend much before they break?

(A) Brittle materials

(B) Ductile materials

(C) Short fiber materials

(D) Heat treated materials

280) How should a structural inspection be performed?

(A) By measuring every crack size

(B) By calculating stress in a slab

(C) By looking for resultant movement

(D) By recommending a structural engineer every time

281) What is one of the most significant causes of house structure problems?

(A) Elastic soils

(B) Expansive soils

(C) Expensive soils

(D) Compacting soils

282) Which of the following is a phenomenon whereby damp soil on the outside of the building will actually freeze to the building and as the soils heave, it will pick up the top part of the foundation wall.

(A) Consolidation

(B) Settlement

(C) Differential settlement

(D) Adfeezing

283) How high should foundations extend above grade?

(A) At least three inches

(B) At least four inches

(C) At least five inches

(D) At least six inches

284) What is commonly found in houses where there is not basement?

(A) Rot

(B) Mat

(C) Piers

(D) Vent pipes

285) Which of the following is not a slab on grade construction type?

(A) Pier

(B) Monolithic

(C) Supported

(D) Floating

286) With slab on grade foundations, none of the foundation is accessible; however, it is possible to detect early signs of problems.

True or False?

287) In new construction, the brick veneer wall sits directly on the:

(A) Foundation

(B) Wood sill

(C) Ground

(D) Framing members

288) Which of the following has a function to carry floor and wall loads horizontally to the foundations, walls, or posts.

(A) Joist

(B) King post

(C) Beam

(D) Lentil

289) Typically, what is considered the minimum end bearing for beams?

(A) 3-3/8 inches

(B) 2-5/8 inches

(C) 3-3/8 inches

(D) 3-5/8 inches

290) Doubling a joist by putting another of the same size beside it will _____ its resistance to bending.

(A) Double

(B) Triple

(C) Quadruple

(D) Weaken

291) Doubling the depth of a joist increases its deflection resistance by how many times?

(A) 2 times

(B) 4 times

(C) 6 times

(D) 8 times

292) What is the function of bridging/bracing between joists?

(A) To restrain from bending

(B) To restrain from buckling

(C) To restrain from twisting

(D) To restrain from sagging

293) Most floor trusses are:

(A) 10 to 18 inches deep

(B) 8 to 12 inches deep

(C) 18 to 24 inches deep

(D) 10 to 15 inches deep

294) How thick are concrete floors typically in modern construction?

(A) 4 inches

(B) 3-1/2 inches

(C) 3 inches

(D) 4-1/2 inches

295) For masonry wall systems, what is a typical problem when the inner and outer wythes are not adequately secured together?

(A) Vertical cracks

(B) Horizontal cracks

(C) Diagonal cracks

(D) The outer wythes can lean or bow outwards

296) Spreading rafter may push the top of the:

(A) Walls inwards

(B) Walls outwards

(C) Walls down and will often buckle

(D) Walls in tension

297) All wiring in a typical house is direct current.

True or False?

298) Most homes are equipped with what type of electrical system:

(A) 110/220 volt

(B) 120/240 volt

(C) 120/220 volt

(D) 110/240 volt

299) All of the following are good insulators, except:

(A) Wood

(B) Silver

(C) Air

(D)Ceramic

300) What will shut off the electricity before a wire will overheat?

(A) Impedance breaker

(B) Socket breaker

(C) Electricity breaker

(D) Fuse or circuit breaker

301) A 900 watt blow dryer when subjected to a potential of 120 volts will allow many amps to flow through it?

(A) .075 amps

(B) 75 amps

(C) .75 amps

(D) 7.5 amps

302) What is the home electrical capability that has a 240 volt power supply with 75 amp main fuses?

(A) 12 kilowatts

(B) 18 kilowatts

(C) 24 kilowatts

(D) 38 kilowatts

303) The amount of current a wire can carry is determined mostly by its:

(A) Brand

(B) Length

(C) Impedance

(D) Diameter

304) Calculate the monthly electric bill for a home which uses 1500 kWh for that month. Assume the electric company charges 10 cents per kWh.

(A) $50

(B) $100

(C) $150

(D) $200

305) What is the advantage of circuit breakers over fuses?

(A) Circuit breakers can be turned back on

(B) Circuit breakers have to be replaced which is inexpensive

(C) Fuses can be turned back on which is troublesome

(D) Circuit breakers are safer than fuses

306) The electrical service entrance to a home typically has how many wires?

(A) 1 wire

(B) 2 wires

(C) 3 wires

(D) 4 wires

307) The utility company should be contacted if the overhead wires of a service drop are less than:

(A) 10 feet above the ground

(B) 12 feet above the ground

(C) 35 feet above the ground

(D) 15 feet above the ground

308) What is the purpose of a drip loop for electrical cable at the service entrance?

(A) To allow the current to flow more efficient

(B) To allow the voltage to flow more efficient

(C) To keep unwanted critters from entering the conduit

(D) To keep water from entering the conduit

309) In a conventional 60-amp service with circuit breakers, the breakers will trip when the current in either leg reaches:

(A) 50 amps

(B) 55 amps

(C) 60 amps

(D) 65 amps

310) The main switch or breaker is normally shut off during a home inspection.

True or False?

311) Where is a safe place to dispose of unwanted electricity.

(A) In the trash

(B) Ground

(C) In the service panel

(D) Ceiling

312) What is the purpose of special di-electric type piping connections?

(A) To allow oxidization

(B) To prevent magnetism

(C) To prevent loose connections

(D) To prevent oxidization

313) What is the name used to describe when circuits in a panel in which are doubled by adding another wire to the terminal screw?

(A) Double tap

(B) Double screw

(C) Double wire

(D) Double connection

314) The wire used to carry electricity from the panels to the fixtures and appliances is typically:

(A) Aluminum

(B) Brass

(C) Silver

(D) Copper

315) If heat is developed by gas, oil, or electricity and is transferred to air, the system is referred to as a:

(A) Boiler

(B) Distribution system

(C) Furnace

(D) Heat pump

316) Electric heaters are best located in this area which tends to have the coolest spot in a room.

(A) Floor level by outside wall above windows

(B) Floor level by inside wall

(C) Floor level by outside wall below windows

(D) Ceiling level by outside wall below windows

317) How high should draperies and curtains be above electric heaters?

(A) 4 inches

(B) 6 inches

(C) 8 inches

(D) 10 inches

318) Which is a common complaint about radiant heating systems?

(A) Radiant effect

(B) Heat effect

(C) Light effect

(D) Shadow effect

319) All of the following are components to furnaces (exception of electric furnaces), except:

(A) Radiant barrier

(B) Burner

(C) Blower

(D) Heat exchanger

320) What is the pressure, typically, in modern boiler piping?

(A) 6 to 9 psi

(B) 8 to 10 psi

(C) 12 to 15 psi

(D) 17 to 21 psi

321) What type of material is a radiator constructed of in a boiler system?

(A) Cast iron

(B) Steel

(C) Aluminum

(D) Ceramic

322) As a general rule, oil-fired furnaces do not require a lined chimney.

True or False?

323) Both furnaces and boilers are classified by their:

 (A) Output

(B) Heat index

(C) Temperature differential

(D) Efficiency

324) Mid efficiency boilers have a seasonal efficiency in this range:

(A) 60%

(B) 70%

(C) 80%

(D) 90%

325) Why is it that the actual condition of a heat exchanger in a boiler or furnace cannot usually be determined during a home inspection?

(A) It would require a special tool

(B) It is not totally visible

(C) It is not a component of a boiler

(D) It is in a hard to reach place

326) Electric furnaces do not have a heat exchanger.

True or False?

327) Gas piping in a home is typically:

(A) Copper or plastic

(B) Black steel or copper

(C) PCV or cast iron

(D) Black steel or PVC

328) Which of the following is often referred to as an "Octopus" furnace?

(A) Forced air furnace

(B) Gravity furnace

(C) Conventional furnace

(D) Electric furnace

329) In a hot water heating system, a leaking or dripping pressure relief valve may mean:

(A) A over pressurized expansion tank

(B) A broken thermocouple

(C) A cracked expansion tank

(D) A waterlogged expansion tank

330) Pressure relief valves are often found on "open" hot water systems.

True or False?

331) When liquids evaporate into gases, they absorb a significant amount of:

(A) Dust particles

(B) Cold air

(C) Heat

(D) Humidity

332) Which of the following is an air conditioner which can work in reverse to help heat the home when cooling is not needed?

(A) Cold pump

(B) Heat pump

(C) Tankless heater

(D) Heat regulator

333) What is the most critical component in a conventional air conditioner?

(A) Freon

(B) Condenser

(C) Compressor

(D) Blower

Exam # 5 Solutions

Solution to Question # 268:

(C) 6 inches.

Solution to Question # 269:

True.

Solution to Question # 270:

(B) Wood framing members shrink in this area.

Solution to Question # 271:

(D) Rounded heads.

Old siding nails have rounded heads which allows the overlapping piece of siding above not sit tightly against the lower piece. This is a practice which has unfortunately disappeared.

Solution to Question # 272:

(B) At least 8 inches.

Solution to Question # 273:

(A) Denting.

Damage sections can be replaced on an individual basis.

Solution to Question # 274:

(D) Rot and attack by insects.

Carpeting should also be avoided on wooden steps as it retains moisture and promotes rot.

Solution to Question # 275:

(B) 4 feet.

This is to prevent frost heaving.

Solution to Question # 276:

(B) Compression and tension.

Solution to Question # 277:

(D) Tension.

Solution to Question # 278:

(A) Compression.

Solution to Question # 279:

(A) Brittle materials.

Ceramic tile is brittle, rope is ductile.

Solution to Question # 280:

(C) By looking for resultant movement.

Most structural components are buried below grade or hidden behind furnishes.

Solution to Question # 281:

(B) Expansive soils.

Some clay soils can expand and contract significantly with different moisture contents and can heave floors and foundations when they get wet. When they dry, they shrink and allow the building to drop.

Solution to Question # 282:

(D) Adfeezing. Horizontal cracks in foundation walls just below grade typify this phenomenon.

Solution to Question # 283:

(D) At least six inches.

Most brick used in residential exterior walls is not designed to be in contact with the soil.

Solution to Question # 284:

(C) Piers.

Solution to Question # 285:

(A) Pier.

Solution to Question # 286:

False.

Solution to Question # 287:

(A) Foundation

The wood sill supports the wood framing but not masonry.

Solution to Question # 288:

(C) Beam.

Solution to Question # 289:

(D) 3-5/8 inches.

Where the end bearing is inadequate, the beam can crush itself or tis support. There is also potential for the beam to slip off its support.

Solution to Question # 290:

(A) Double.

Solution to Question # 291:

(D) 8 times. The strength of a joist comes mostly from its depth. Two 2x10's are more resistant to deflection than four 2x8's.

Solution to Question # 292:

(C) To restrain from twisting.

Solution to Question # 293:

(A) 10 to 18 inches deep.

As a general rule of thumb, trusses are 1/12 to 1/20 the depth of its span.

Solution to Question # 294:

(C) 3 inches

Concrete floors in residential construction are usually not structural.

Solution to Question # 295:

(D) The outer wythes can lean or bow outwards.

Solution to Question # 296:

(B) Walls outwards.

This results in a very unstable condition.

Solution to Question # 297:

False.

Alternating current is the correct answer.

Solution to Question # 298:

(B) 120/240 volt.

It can provide 240 volts or 120 volts.

Solution to Question # 299:

(B) Silver.

Silver is a very good conductor. Air is a very good insulator.

Solution to Question # 300:

(D) Fuse or circuit breaker.

Solution to Question # 301:

(D) 7.5 amps.

Remember the $P = IV$, therefore, $900 = I (120)$, so $I = 900/120$, $I = 7.5$ amps.

Solution to Question # 302:

(B) 18 kilowatts.

$P = IV$, therefore, $P = (75)(240) = 18,000$ watts. One kilowatt is equal to 1000 watts. S0, 18000 watts = 18 kilowatts.

Solution to Question # 303:

(D) Diameter.

A larger wire can carry more current. Normal household circuits are designed to carry 15 amps, and #14 gauge wire can do this safely.

Solution to Question # 304:

(C) $150.

Kilowatt-Hour(kWh) is the measure of electricity consumption. The electric meter records kilowatt hours used. Price = kWh used (cost per kWh), therefore, 1500 kWh ($.1) = $150. Remember that 10 cents - $.01 dollars.

Solution to Question # 305:

(A) Circuit breakers can be turned back on.

Fuses have to be replaced.

Solution to Question # 306:

(C) 3 wires.

Red and black wires are live and the white wire is neutral.

Solution to Question # 307:

(D) 15 feet above the ground.

Solution to Question # 308:

(D) To keep water from entering the conduit.

The wires form a loop which allows water to drip off the wire, and not run along into the conduit.

Solution to Question # 309:

(C) 60 amps.

Solution to Question # 310:

False.

It is normally not shut off because it can result in damage to motors, compressors, computers, clocks, etc. You should recommend to the homeowner r to test it once he moves in the home in order to verify that it is working correctly.

Solution to Question # 311:

(B) Ground.

A ground wire connects an electrical system to the ground.

Solution to Question # 312:

(D) To prevent oxidization.

Where two different metals are joined, they prevent oxidization which can lead to corrosion.

Solution to Question # 313:

(A) Double tap.

This is not permitted unless a special connector, designed to hold two wires, is provided.

Solution to Question # 314:

(D) Copper.

Solution to Question # 315:

(C) Furnace.

A boiler uses water as the heat transfer medium

Solution to Question # 316:

(C) Floor level by outside wall below windows.

Solution to Question # 317:

(C) 8 inches.

They should also be 3 inches in front of the heaters as long as they at least 1 inch above the floor.

Solution to Question # 318:

(D) Shadow effect.

The shadow effect is similar to how sunlight works. People can sometimes feel cold, especially their legs, while sitting a table. Their legs are shaded underneath the table and not subject to the direct radiant heat.

Solution to Question # 319:

(A) Radiant barrier.

The heat exchanger is the most critical component of a furnace.

Solution to Question # 320:

(C) 12 to 15 psi.

The pressure within the system is normally a few pounds higher than what is required to force water up o the highest level within the home.

Solution to Question # 321:

(A) Cast iron.

Solution to Question # 322:

True.

This is because the products of combustion are not as corrosive as the products of combustion from a gas-fired system.

Solution to Question # 323:

(D) Efficiency.

Solution to Question # 324:

(C) 80%.

Solution to Question # 325:

(B) It is not totally visible.

There could be a crack or a hole in the heat exchanger that you cannot see.

Solution to Question # 326:

True.

They contain electric heating elements and controls.

Solution to Question # 327:

(B) Black steel or copper. Leaks can create an explosive hazard and should be treated as an emergency safety concern. You should vacate the house immediately.

Solution to Question # 328:

(B) Gravity furnace.

This is because of the large round ductwork that emanates from the furnace body.

Solution to Question # 329:

(D) A waterlogged expansion tank.

Since air in the expansion tank get absorbed into the water over time, the tank has to be drained to prevent it from getting waterlogged.

Solution to Question # 330:

False.

Open systems or not pressurized. This is common in older homes where the expansion tank is located on the upper floor above the level of the radiator.

Solution to Question # 331:

(C) Heat.

Solution to Question # 332:

(B) Heat pump.

This happens by simply reversing the flow of the refrigerant. The condenser becomes the evaporator and the evaporator becomes the condenser.

Solution to Question # 333:

(C) Compressor.

It is the heart of the system. It can be thought of as simply a pump for gases.

334) Modern heat pumps have a Co-efficient of Performance (COP) greater than:

(A) .5

(B) 1.0

(C) 1.5

(D) -1.0

335) From a durability standpoint, most cooling/heat pump installers say it is generally better to slightly oversize a cooling system.

True or False?

336) If an air conditioning compressor is turned on when the outside air is below which of the following temperatures, severe damage can occur.

(A) 40 °F

(B) 50 °F

(C) 60 °F

(D) 70 °F

337) On an air conditioning system, which of the following is used to transfer heat from the house air to the refrigerator within the coil?

(A) Compressor

(B) Evaporator coil

(C) Radiator

(D) Polit light

338) What is the function of the thin fins that are on air conditioning evaporator coils?

(A) To minimize condensation

(B) To minimize heat transfer

(C) To enhance flow of liquid

(D) To enhance heat transfer

339) What is the function of the outdoor fan in an air conditioning system?

(A) To move refrigerate over the outdoor coil

(B) To move air over the outdoor coil

(C) To move liquid over the outdoor condenser

(D) To move gas over the outdoor coil

340) During a home inspection, you observe water stains on top of the furnace. What can this indicate?

(A) Cracked condensate tray

(B) Cracked heat exchanger

(C) Cracked suction line

(D) Cracked liquid line

341) What is the name of the refrigerate line which contains cold vapor and should be insulated to prevent condensation from forming?

(A) Liquid line

(B) Compressor line

(C) Condensation line

(D) Suction line

342) The location of the thermostat is not critical and be placed anywhere.

True or False?

343) On water cooled air conditioning systems, waste water can be used for watering the lawn or filling a swimming pool.

True or False?

344) As a rule of thumb, how long should you wait in-between operating the heating system and operating the cooling system?

(A) 15 minutes

(B) 45 minutes

(C) 1 hour

(D) 2 hours

345) Evaporative coolers do not work well when the outside air is:

(A) Hot

(B) Humid

(C) Cold

(D) Dry

346) What is required on the warm side on most insulations?

(A) Weather stripping

(B) Air barrier

(C) Vapor barrier

(D) Ventilation tab

347) Which side of the insulation should be ventilated to remove the moisture laden air which leaks into the insulation.

(A) Warm side

(B) Middle

(C) Does not need to be ventilated

(D) Cold side

348) Which of the following slows the rate of heat loss from a home?

(A) Radiator

(B) Humidifier

(C) Insulation

(D) Vapor barrier

349) It is common to omit soffit vents if gable vents are installed at opposite ends of the attic.

True or False?

350) When insulating an unused attic area, the goal is to have the temperature in the attic at what temperature as compared to the outdoor temperature?

(A) Greater than

(B) Less than

(C) Slightly greater than

(D) The same

351) Roof vents rely on which of the following heat transfer methods to allow warm air to escape from higher vents and cool air to enter into the lower vents?

(A) Conduction

(B) Convection

(C) Radiation

(D) Attic fan

352) It is impossible to install an air/vapor barrier without providing a new ceiling surface.

True or False?

353) Which of the following is a vertical wall commonly found in 1-1/2 or 2-1/2 story homes and separates the top floor living space from the side attic areas?

(A) Shear wall

(B) Separator wall

(C) Transient wall

(D) Knee wall

354) Masonry walls can be insulated by providing a false wall on the interior or exterior of the existing wall.

True or False?

355) Most of the heat loss in buildings with log walls is by:

(A) Air infiltration

(B) Humidity levels

(C) Convection

(D) Radiant barrier

356) Which of the following is a numerical representation of thermal resistance?

(A) S-value

(B) T-value

(C) Q-value

(D) R-value

357) Retrofitting wall insulation in masonry homes is very cost-effective.

True or False?

358) Log walls are solid and provide no means of insulating inside of the wall.

True or False?

359) Many houses in urban and suburban area are provided with water by the town normally supplied at how much pressure?

(A) 40 to 70 psi

(B) 30 to 45 psi

(C) 20 to 45 psi

(D) 65 to 90 psi

360) Which of the following piping material is used today for almost all supply lines from the city main to the home?

(A) Galvanized steel

(B) Lead

(C) Copper

(D) Plastic

361) What should be provided to prevent leaks at fixtures when the municipal water pressure is above 80 psi?

(A) Accumulator

(B) Regulation

(C) Regression valve

(D) Regulator

362) The service piping for a water wall is most often:

(A) Plastic

(B) Copper

(C) Galvanized steel

(D) Lead

363) Which of the following piping materials was used almost exclusively up to about 1950?

(A) Copper

(B) Galvanized steel

(C) Plastic

(D) Lead

364) How can brass piping be identified?

(A) Smooth fittings

(B) Spiral welded fittings

(C) Lack of fittings

(D) Threaded fittings

365) Galvanized steel piping will often leak first at the:

(A) Welds

(B) Outside pipe wall

(C) Middle part of a pipe run

(D) Joints

366) What is often used when copping piping and steel piping are joined?

(A) Special connectors

(B) Special gaskets

(C) Special booster pumps

(D) Special weld procedure

367) Which of the following materials has become almost exclusively used for waste plumbing since 1960?

(A) Copper

(B) ABS plastic pipe

(C) Galvanized steel

(D) Lead

368) Which of the following material was used to waste plumbing up until the 1950s?

(A) Plastic

(B) Galvanized steel

(C) Copper

(D) Lead

369) What is the recommended slope for waste plumbing pipes?

(A) 5/8 inch per foot

(B) ½ inch per foot

(C) ¼ inch per foot

(D) 3/8 inch per foot

370) What is the purpose of a trap in plumbing fixtures?

(A) To prevent corrosion

(B) For better water flow

(C) To help siphoning

(D) To prevent sewer odors from coming in

371) Two traps are sometimes permitted on plumbing fixtures.

True or False?

372) For water to drain freely out of a house waste system, there must be adequate:

(A) Pipe diameter

(B) Venting

(C) Fittings

(D) Insulation

373) Wastewater vents must extend how many feet above the roof line?

(A) 3 inches

(B) 6 inches

(C) 10 inches

(D) 12 inches

374) What is the most common problem on interior finishes?

(A) Termite damage

(B) Water damage

(C) Paint flaking

(D) Poor workmanship

375) In new construction, how think is typically a concrete basement floor?

(A) At least 2 inches

(B) At least 5 inches

(C) At least 4 ½ inches

(D) At least 3 inches

376) Hardwood flooring can be used without any subflooring as long as the hardwood is how think?

(A) ¾ inch thick or more

(B) ½ inch thick or more

(C) 1 inch thick or more

(D) ¼ inch thick or more

377) Hardwood flooring should be installed parallel to the subflooring.

True or False?

378) Which of the following is the most common subflooring?

(A) Pine

(B) Oak

(C) Laminate

(D) Redwood

379) Squeaky floors usually indicate a structural problem.

True or False?

380) A subfloor usually squeaks when walked on because the flooring finish or subfloor is:

(A) Over spanned and may collapse

(B) Not secured tightly to the floor joists below

(C) New and requires to be broken in

(D) Rotted

381) Building codes require that ceramic tile be set in at least:

(A) 1 ¼ inches of mortar

(B) ¼ inches of mortar

(C) 2 ¼ inches of mortar

(D) 1 ¾ inches of mortar

382) The most common problem with ceramic tiling is:

(A) Buckling

(B) Ungluing

(C) Scratching

(D) Cracking

383) Drywall is commonly available in all of the following thicknesses, except:

(A) 3/8 inch

(B) ½ inch

(C) ¼ inch

(D) 5/8 inch

384) A common problem with plaster applied over gypsum lath is the:

(A) Sagging effect

(B) Fire effect

(C) Shape effect

(D) Shadow/bulge effect

385) What are the three layers of plaster called:

(A) Brown, scratch, and finish

(B) Putty, brown, and finish

(C) Scratch, brown, and finish

(D) Scratch, putty, and brown

386) For stair railings, a good rule of thumb is no openings larger than:

(A) 2 inches in diameter

(B) 3 inches in diameter

(C) 4 inches in diameter

(D) 8 inches in diameter

387) In traditional window systems, what is used to hold the glass in the sash?

(A) Special glue

(B) Glazing compound or putty

(C) Plastic clips

(D) Metal clips

388) What is the process called in which glass is strengthened?

(A) Annealing

(B) Economizing

(C) Tempering

(D) Crystallization

389) You can always identify a failed seal in a window during a home inspection.

True or False?

390) The most common problem with the head of a window is:

(A) A sagging lintel

(B) A broken seal

(C) Condensation

(D) Trapped moisture

391) Doors should have a step up from the outdoors to the door sill of about:

(A) 1 inch

(B) 2 inches

(C) 4 inches

(D) 6 inches

392) The slope of a smoke chamber should not be more than 45 degrees off vertical and should slope evenly from both sides.

True or False?

393) For a home homeowner, a home inspection is designed to:

(A) Give you an insurance policy

(B) Eliminate all risks

(C) Be technically exhaustive

(D) Better your odds

394) In a roof truss, the top and bottom chords are called:

(A) Webs

(B) Gusset plates

(C) Chords

(D) Members

395) Which of the following terms performs the same function as a lintel- to redirect the load above an opening in a masonry wall to the solid wall sections on either side.

(A) Arch

(B) Gussct plates

(C) Column

(D) Ledger

396) Houses built on sloping lots are not prone to footing and foundation failures as a level lot.

True or False?

397) The heavier the building and weaker the soil, the smaller the footing should be.

True or False.

398) Steel is good in tension but weak in compression.

True or False?

399) During a home inspection, the results of footing failure can usually be seen.

True or False?

400) What term is used to describe the potential energy of an electrical system.

(A) Amps

(B) Voltage

(C) Wattage

(D) Impedance

Solution to Exam # 6:

Solution to Question # 334:

(B) 1.0.

Typically down to -25 ºF

Solution to Question # 335:

False.

The equipment will last longer if it is slightly undersized.

Solution to Question # 336:

(C) 60 ºF.

Solution to Question # 337:

(B) Evaporator coil.

Also known as a plenum coil.

Solution to Question # 338:

(D) To enhance heat transfer.

Fins on dinosaurs also help them cool off by enhancing heat transfer. Finds provide more surface areas for heat transfer.

Solution to Question # 339:

(B) To move air over the outdoor coil.

This cools the refrigerant during the cooling mode and adds heat in the heating mode.

Solution to Question # 340:

(A) Cracked condensate tray. It can also mean a tray which is not level, or a tray which is plugged and is overflowing.

Solution to Question # 341:

(D) Suction line.

Solution to Question # 342:

False.

The location is very critical and should never be exposed to drafts, sunlight, and heating/cooling sources.

Solution to Question # 343:

True.

The wastewater is non-potable, which means non-drinkable and cannot be used as drinking water. However, you can use it to water your lawn or fill the swimming pool.

Solution to Question # 344:

(A) 15 minutes.

Solution to Question # 345:

(B) Humid.

Since the inside air ends up being humid as well, it can lead to mold and bacteria problems.

Solution to Question # 346:

(C) Vapor barrier.

Some insulations are not permeable and do not require it. Air in the insulation can cool to the point that it deposits moisture into the insulation and must be protected against.

Solution to Question # 347:

(D) Cold side.

This allows moisture to be carried out of the building quickly.

Solution to Question # 348:

(C) Insulation.

The best insulating materials are light weight

Solution to Question # 349:

True.

Solution to Question # 350:

(D) The same.

Some people think that it should be the same temperature as the warm house in order to work correctly. This is incorrect. Also, the insulation should be installed on the floor of the attic, not the attic ceiling.

Solution to Question # 351:

(B) Convection.

Solution to Question # 352:

True.

Solution to Question # 353:

(D) Knee wall.

Solution to Question # 354:

True.

Solution to Question # 355:

(A) Air infiltration.

Sealing leaks is more cost effective than adding wall insulation.

Solution to Question # 356:

(D) R-value.

The higher the number, the greater resistance to heat transfer.

Solution to Question # 357:

False.

Solution to Question # 358:

True.

Solution to Question # 359:

(A) 40 to 70 psi.

Solution to Question # 360:

(C) Copper.

Most source piping since 1970 is ¾ inch diameter and has an indefinite life expectancy.

Solution to Question # 361:

(D) Regulator.

Solution to Question # 362:

(A) Plastic.

Solution to Question # 363:

(B) Galvanized steel.

This piping can last 40 to 60 years.

Solution to Question # 364:

(D) Threaded fittings.

Brass piping is an alloy of copper and tin and it cannot attract a magnet.

Solution to Question # 365:

(D) Joints.

Where it joins a fitting, it has threads cut into it. The pipe wall is thinner at these threaded connections.

Solution to Question # 366:

(A) Special connectors.

To prevent galvanic reaction. The special dielectric connectors separate the metals and reduce deterioration.

Solution to Question # 367:

(B) ABS plastic pipe.

It is used for drains, wastes and vents and is connected by using plastic cement (glue).

Solution to Question # 368:

(D) Lead.

It was used because of its resistance to corrosion and it's workability. However, lead is prone to leakage at the connections.

Solution to Question # 369:

(C) ¼ inch per foot.

Solution to Question # 370:

(D) To prevent sewer odors from coming in.

Solution to Question # 371:

False.

This arrangement can produce chronic blockage.

Solution to Question # 372:

(B) Venting.

Solution to Question # 373:

(B) 6 inches.

And also must be 12 inches away from any wall.

Solution to Question # 374:

(B) Water damage.

Water damage may be on floors, walls, or ceilings.

Solution to Question # 375:

(D) At least 3 inches.

The floor should be sloped to down to a floor drain.

Solution to Question # 376:

(B) ½ inch thick or more.

Solution to Question # 377:

False.

Solution to Question # 378:

(A) Pine.

Pine floors are usually used as finish flooring in a ¼ tongue and groove configuration or as a subfloor.

Solution to Question # 379:

False.

Solution to Question # 380:

(B) Not secured tightly to the floor joists below.

The squeaking is commonly the result of the nails sliding in and out of the nail holes.

Solution to Question # 381:

(A) 1 ¼ inches of mortar.

And also that a 2x2 inch galvanized wire mesh be used in the mortar bed.

Solution to Question # 382:

(D) Cracking.

This is usually the result of a floor system which is not stiff enough to support the tile.

Solution to Question # 383:

(C) ¼ inch.

Solution to Question # 384:

(D) Shadow/bulge effect.

This can be created when the plaster is applied too quickly and the finish coat is applied before the first coat dried completely.

Solution to Question # 385:

(C) Scratch, brown, and finish.

The third coat is called the "finish" or "putty" coat.

Solution to Question # 386:

(C) 4 inches in diameter.

Solution to Question # 387:

(B) Glazing compound or putty.

Solution to Question # 388:

(C) Tempering.

Fully tempered glass is made three to five times stronger than ordinary glass by heating and cooling it very fast.

Solution to Question # 389:

False.

Solution to Question # 390:

(A) Sagging lintel.

If the lintel beam above the window opening is not strong enough, the window may be deflected and thus the window cannot operate.

Solution to Question # 391:

(D) 6 inches.

If there is not 6 inch step up, then regular maintenance is required in order to prevent serious water damage.

Solution to Question # 392:

True.

The side walls of a smoke chamber are designed to slope to direct the smoke from the wide damper opening into the narrow chimney flue.

Solution to Question # 393:

(D) Better your odds.

Home inspectors are considered generalists and not specialists.

Solution to Question # 394:

(C) Chords.

Solution to Question # 395:

(A) An arch.

Solution to Question # 396:

False.

Solution to Question # 397:

False.

The larger the footing should be.

Solution to Question # 398:

False.

Steel is good in tension and compression

Solution to Question # 399:

True.

However, it is difficult to know whether the building is still moving at the time of inspection.

Solution to Question # 400:

(B) Voltage.

A large electrical voltage means that a large potential electric force is available.

"Everything starts with the basic fundamentals and the willingness to work hard and practice good habits".

- Cal Ripken Sr.

Made in the USA
Middletown, DE
02 November 2023

41809161R00129